Wörterbuch soziale Arbeit

Deutsch – Englisch
Englisch – Deutsch

Verfasser: Peter Herrmann

Eigenverlag des Deutschen Vereins
für öffentliche und private Fürsorge e.V.
Berlin

Wörterbuch soziale Arbeit

Deutsch – Englisch Englisch – Deutsch

Mit einem Glossar wichtiger Begriffe aus der sozialen Arbeit
in Deutschland und England

Von Peter Herrmann

Eigenverlag des Deutschen Vereins
für öffentliche und private Fürsorge e.V.,
Michaelkirchstraße 17/18, 10179 Berlin

Printed in Germany 2002
Unveränderter Nachdruck 2008

Die Auslieferung an den Buchhandel und an Nichtmitglieder des Deutschen Vereins
erfolgt über den Lambertus Verlag, Freiburg, www.lambertus.de

ISBN 978-3-7841-1766-9

Veröffentlicht mit Förderung durch das Bundesministerium für Familie, Senioren,
Frauen und Jugend (BMFSFJ)

Inhalt

Vorwort

Zu den Leitthemen, mit denen sich der Deutsche Verein in Zukunft verstärkt befassen wird, gehören auch Fragen der europäischen Einigung und Integration. Die Aufmerksamkeit wird sich dabei insbesondere auf Fragen der sozialen Sicherung, der Sozialpolitik und der sozialen Arbeit insgesamt richten. Im Prozess der europäischen Einigung, besonders in der Folge des Vertrages von Nizza und der Charta der europäischen Grundrechte, gewinnen internationale Fachdiskussionen und Abstimmungsprozesse immer stärker an Bedeutung.

Besonderes Gewicht haben in dieser Entwicklung seit jeher internationale Austauschprogramme und Begegnungen, Fachkongresse sowie die Lektüre von Fachliteratur. Zur Unterstützung der daran beteiligten Fach- und Leitungskräfte von öffentlichen und freien Trägern und Nichtregierungsorganisationen sowie von Politikern unterschiedlicher staatlicher Ebenen hatte der Deutsche Verein bereits 1988 ein deutsch-englisches *Wörterbuch der sozialen Arbeit* herausgegeben.

Nun liegt eine vollständig überarbeitete Neuauflage vor, die von Dr. Peter Herrmann bearbeitet und mit Unterstützung des Bundesministeriums für Familie, Senioren, Frauen und Jugend hergestellt wurde.

Dafür sagen wir unseren besonderen Dank und hoffen, dass dieses Wörterbuch auf gleiches Interesse treffen wird wie die erste Ausgabe.

Frankfurt am Main,
im November 2002

Dr. Konrad Deufel – Vorsitzender des Deutschen Vereins
Michael Löher – Geschäftsführer des Deutschen Vereins

Preface

In the future the *Deutsche Verein* will more and more be challenged to take topics in the context of European unification and integration into account. Questions concerned with social security, social policy and more in general social work will be of particular importance. As part of the process of European unification and especially as consequence of the Treaty of Nice and the Charta of European Fundamental Rights international debates and coordinating actions are getting more and more important.

It is well known from previous developments that as part of such a development international exchange programmes and gatherings, congresses on important contemporary topics and as well the reading of relevant documents is gathering momentum. The *Deutsche Verein* edited already in 1988 a *German-English Dictionary of Social Work* in order to support the staff involved – managers and key figures from public and private bodies and nongovernmental organisations, politicians at various levels.

We are glad to be able to present a completely revised edition – edited by Dr. Peter Herrmann produced with the support of the Federal Ministry for Family Affairs, Senior Citizens, Women and Youth.

We say Thank You for the efforts involved and hope that the dictionary will be met with the same interest as the first edition.

Frankfurt am Main,
im November 2002

Dr. Konrad Deufel – Vorsitzender des Deutschen Vereins
Michael Löher – Geschäftsführer des Deutschen Vereins

Einführung

Technische Hinweise

📖 Verweis auf Begriffe im Glossar

⇒ Verweis auf andere Begriffe im jeweiligen Wörterbuchteil, i.e. innerhalb des Deutsch-Englischen, Englisch-Deutschen Übersetzungsabschnitts oder innerhalb des Glossars.

Einige allgemeine Anmerkungen scheinen vorab noch sinnvoll zur weiteren Benutzung – die Vorgehensweise entspricht nahezu vollständig derjenigen des Fachlexikons, welches ebenfalls vom Deutschen Verein für öffentliche und private Fürsorge herausgegeben wird.

Die Begriffe sind alphabetisch angeordnet; die Umlaute ä, ö und ü werden wie ihre Grundlaute a, o und u. Der Buchstabe ß ist wie ss eingeordnet. Der Konvention für Lexika entsprechend werden Leer- und Sonderzeichen nicht bei der alphabetischen Ordnung berücksichtigt.

Eine Ausnahme der alphabetischen Sortierung erfolgt im Anhang – Gesetzestitel, Deklarationen und andere Dokumente sind im Grossen und Ganzen alphabetisch angeordnet, soweit sie allerdings eindeutig bestimmten Institutionen zuzuordnen sind (etwa dem Europarat, der Internationalen Arbeitsorganisation sowie den Vereinten Nationen diesen Organisationen), sind sie unter den jeweiligen Organisationsnamen zugeordnet.

Im Glossar findet sich keine eins-zu-eins-Übersetzung. Die Erläuterungen sind mit wenigen Ausnahmen in derjenigen Sprache angeführt, in der sie "Sinn" machen, d.h. in der am ehesten Erläuterungsbedarf besteht.

Folgende Abkürzungen sind verwendet:

A – Österreich
D – Deutschland
Jur. – Juristisch
Med. – Medizinisch
Päd. – Pädagogisch/Pädagogik
Psych. – Psychologisch/Psychologie
Soz. – Soziologisch/Soziologie/sozial
UK – Vereinigtes Königreich
US – Vereinigte Staaten von Amerika

Zum Projekt

Wenngleich es sich hier um ein traditionelles Wörterbuch handelt, so ist doch zugleich die Verwirklichung eines anderen Zieles damit angestrebt. Es handelt sich um Begriffe, die sich als besonders relevant für jene zeigen, die mit Begriffen des Sozialwesens und deren Entwicklung befasst sind. Es handelt ich hier um eine revidierte Fassung des Wörterbuches *Soziale Arbeit. Deutsch – Englisch, Englisch – Deutsch aus dem Jahr 1988 (Hrsg.: Deutscher Verein für öffentliche und private Fürsorge, Frankfurt/M./ 1988).*

Eine Änderung ist darin zu sehen, dass wir hier nicht ausschließlich auf den Bereich Sozialer Arbeit zielen, wie es der Titel vorschlagen mag. Selbst in jener Ausgabe war ja der Begriff der sozialen Arbeit weit gefasst. Tatsache ist, dass der Blick auf die verschiedenen Teildisziplinen des Sozialen mehr und mehr verschwimmt. Um dem Rechnung zu tragen, hat das hier vorgelegte Büchlein einen neuen Charakter, nämlich den eines Wörterbuchs *sozialer Begriffe.* Freilich wird damit weder der Anspruch auf Ausschließlichkeit erhoben, noch jener auf Vollständigkeit.

Was als Übersetzung eines jeweiligen Begriffs angegeben ist, gibt nicht unbedingt die vollständige Bandbreite der möglichen Übersetzungen wieder. So ist beispielsweise für den Begriff *atomised vereinzelt, zersplittert* angegeben, nicht aber *zerstäubt* – eine Bedeutung, die für unseren Bereich nicht relevant erscheint. Wir sind hier an bestimmten Bedeutungen interessiert und nicht an der sprachlichen Seite. So ist vielfach auch ein Begriff als Verb genannt, nicht aber als Nomen (oder umgekehrt).

Die Überarbeitung des Ursprungsdokumentes hat auch einige interessante allgemeine Fragen zum Vorschein gebracht, die mit der Tatsache zusammenhängen, dass Sprache etwas Lebendes ist, etwas, was eine eigene Entwicklung aufweist, was aber auch stark die gesellschaftlichen Entwicklungen widerspiegelt. Dies geht so weit, dass einige Begriffe nur im Glossar ausgewiesen sind, da sie vollständig “neu kreiert“ zu sein scheinen – so konnte nicht einfach eine Übersetzung dargeboten werden, sondern es war die Einführung eines neuen Begriffes erforderlich. Der Begriff der *communitisation* mag als Beispiel stehen.

Was sich allgemein als spannend erweist ist, welche Begriffe denn nun aufgenommen werden sollen. Diese Änderungen – Ergänzungen ebenso wie Streichungen – reflektieren den Wandel sozialprofessioneller Herangehensweisen ebenso wie einen institutionellen und staatlichen Wandel. So ist ein Grossteil der Begriffe aus dem Management, der allgemeinen Verwaltung und aus dem Zusammenhang von Sparmassnahmen aufgenommen.

Ein anderer Punkt in diesem Zusammenhang besteht darin, dass einige Begriffe hinfällig geworden sind – teils sind sie politisch inkorrekt oder fragwürdig, was bedeutsam ist, da ja die Bedeutung der Sprache als politisches und soziales Medium allgemein immer bewusster wird. Außerdem muss von einem Zwischenbereich ausgegangen werden: Begriffe wurden lange Zeit für etwas verwendet, was heutigen Vorstellungen zuwiderläuft. Ein typisches Beispiel ist hier die Psychohygiene – als Mittel der vollständigen Kontrolle und Unterordnung wurde es während des Faschismus weitgehend missbraucht. Gleichwohl ist der Begriff auch heute noch aktuell und wird – wenn auch mit anderer Bedeutung – von der Weltgesundheitsorganisation verwendet.

So hat also schon die Auflistung der Begriffe eine weitgehend paradigmatische Dimension und geht weit über die Übersetzung hinaus.

Bei der Auflistung dienten die vorhandenen und zurate gezogenen Wörterbücher nur als Anregung. Umgekehrt besteht das Ziel des vorliegenden Dokumentes nicht darin, jene Bücher zu ersetzen, und wichtige Begriffe wurden hier nicht einfach wiederholt. Kriterium für die Aufnahme eines Begriffes war zum einen, eine Hilfestellung bei immer wieder auftauchenden Übersetzungsproblemen zu geben – Problemen, die ich selbst erfahren habe oder die immer wieder auf Arbeitstreffen, Konferenzen etc. auftauchten. Zum Zweiten sollten Begriffe aufgenommen werden, die sich erst in jüngerer Zeit als besonders relevant für den Sozialbereich erwiesen haben.

Die Übersetzung hängt somit auch sehr stark von der jeweiligen Schule oder dem jeweiligen Arbeitszusammenhang ab. Dies wird deutlich, wenn wir beispielsweise verschiedene Übersetzungsmöglichkeiten in Erwägung ziehen, die sich für den Begriff *Milieu (Umgebung)* ergeben: *milieu, social environment, social setting* – es ließen sich auch noch andere Möglichkeiten anführen. Manchmal kann es helfen, bei der Suche nach einem wirklich passenden Begriff für die Übersetzung ein Wörterbuch sinnverwandter Begriffe zu Hilfe zu nehmen. Aber hier sollte man immer gewahr sein, dass eine scheinbare Entsprechung nur oberflächlich zutrifft und am Ende zu Missverständnissen führen kann. Rehabilitation, wie es in vielen Ländern scheinbar gleich verwendet wird, hat sehr unterschiedliche Bedeutungen, wenn es zu wichtigen Detailfragen kommt.

Wie auch immer – so weitreichend all dies klingen mag, so bleibt es am Ende doch nur ein kleines Hilfsmittel für jene, die mehrsprachig im Sozialbereich arbeiten.

Eine weitere Bemerkung ist hinsichtlich der sprachlichen Orientierung anzufügen. Generell ist auf das British-English in der Schreibweise aufgebaut, was sich einfach aus pragmatischen Gründen ergibt. Dies hat aber auch einen inhaltlichen Hintergrund, denn innerhalb der EU sollte dies *die* Englische Sprache sein, und nicht die Variante des US-Amerikanischen (hierzu muss man kein Sprachpuritaner sein). Was aber wichtiger ist, ist die Tatsache, dass die Begriffe, die hier relevant sind, eben trotz aller Einflüsse aus dem US-Amerikanischen zumeist in der britischen Tradition stehen. Ohne dies im Detail auszuführen, müssen wir die Bedeutung der englischen Tradition hervorheben, die sich im Bereich sozialer Berufe findet. Dies bedeutet nicht, dass andere Traditionen unwichtig sind. Der Hinweis ist nur darauf bezogen, dass es eben letztlich eher die britische und nicht die amerikanische Tradition ist, die eine Rolle spielt. Dies gilt zumindest heute noch, auch wenn die Prozesse der Globalisierung hier eine Änderung ergeben mögen. Aber es ist immer auch zu berücksichtigen, dass Kontakte über den Atlantik hinweg schon früh für soziale Berufe kennzeichnend waren.

Die Entscheidung, welche Sprache als Ausgangspunkt genommen werden sollte, war freilich schon stark durch das Ursprungswerk, das Wörterbuch von 1988 gegeben und dies bedeutete, dass es die deutsche Sprache war. Jüngere Entwicklungen stellten aber eine Versuchung dar, vom Englischen auszugehen und in dieser Hinsicht den Wortstamm zu revidieren. Inhaltlich besteht der Grund darin, bestimmte Teildisziplinen auf diese Weise enger zusammenzubringen. Dies bedeutet insbesondere die Anerkennung der Eigenständigkeit der drei Hauptstränge, namentlich der *Gemeinwesenarbeit,* der *Sozialarbeit* und *Sozialpolitik.* Eine solche Anerkennung der Selbstständigkeit erlaubt – paradoxerweise – zugleich eine größere gegenseitige Integration der Wissenschaften. In der deutschen Tradition führt die recht strenge Unterordnung der *Gemeinwesenarbeit* unter die *Sozialarbeit* zur Leugnung der Bedeutung der einzelnen Subjekte, i.e. *Gemeinwesenarbeit* und *Sozialarbeit (🕮 social intervention).* In diesem Sinn kann man wohl auch von einer Anerkennung der britischen Tradition in Europa sprechen. Diese Aussage schließt die Interpretation ein, dass *social work* in der britischen Tradition auf der anderen Seite *social pedagogies* aufgesogen hat – eine Teildisziplin, die in Deutschland nach wie vor eine recht starke Unabhängigkeit aufweist.

All dies schließt ein, dass der Nutzer des Wörterbuches das Wörterbuch dazu verwenden kann, Texte in englischer Sprache besser selbst zu übersetzen, d.h. im Original verstehen zu können. Außerdem ist ja auch in der hiesigen Alltagssprache jeweils das *british-english* der Bezugspunkt auf Konferenzen oder im Fachkontakt bei Austauschprogrammen (freilich, dieses *british-english* ist in vielen Fällen mehr *Pidgin-English* als irgendetwas anderes).

Natürlich kann hier kein Sprachkurs angehängt werden. Eine Bemerkung sei jedoch erlaubt. In der deutschen Sprache ist es eine Gewohnheit, einzelne Wörter zu Begriffen zu verbinden und Mammute zu bilden. Und es besteht auch ein Trend, dies dann in die englische Sprache zu übertragen. Insbesondere in den Bereichen des sozialen Handelns ist dies eine allgemein übliche Vorgehensweise, da wir es hier mit komplexen Zusammenhängen zu tun haben, oft mit multidimensionalen Prozessen, die natürlich die Begriffskombination gleichsam herausfordert. Und es ist festzustellen, dass ein solcher Trend auch zunehmend bei Personen zu finden ist, deren Muttersprache Englisch ist. Gleichwohl ist es korrekter, eine "verborientierte" Sprache zu verwenden, d.h. sich auch sprachlich daran zu orientieren, Prozesse zu erfassen und zu beschreiben, anstatt Strukturen festzustellen. So ist es beispielsweise angemessener, *"reconciliation of (the) family, ~ of family members"* zu verwenden anstatt von *"family reconciliation"* zu sprechen. Zugleich ist aber festzuhalten, dass es in vielen Fällen einfach vom persönlichen Geschmack und Stil, und ebenso vom akademischen Zusammenhang, von Traditionen und regionalen Besonderheiten abhängt, welche Ausdrucksweise man verwendet. Insbesondere mit der Vermischung von Sprachen und dem Pidgin-Englisch verbreitet sich die Verwendung von Begriffsungetümen. Gleichwohl sollte beachtet werden, was zuvor gesagt wurde: die Verwendung von Verben als Reflektion von Prozessen und die Verwendung von Nomina als Ausdruck einer Orientierung an Strukturen. Und natürlich bringt uns dies zurück zu dem, was bereits in anderem Zusammenhang gesagt wurde: Sprache ist nicht starr, sondern entwickelt sich, sie "lebt".

Quellen

Die Angaben, die im Folgenden aufgelistet sind, haben sich als wichtige Hilfsmittel erwiesen – dies gilt mit Blick auf die Stichwörterauswahl ebenso wie mit Blick auf Überlegungen bei der Übersetzung.

* Halbach, Günter et altera: Labour Law in Germany: an overview, Ed.: Federal Ministry of Labour and Social Affairs, Bonn 1994[5]

* Bauer, Rudolph (Ed.): Lexikon des Sozial- und Gesundheitswesens, München/Wien: R. Oldenbourg Verlag, 1992
* Wörterbuch für Sozialberufe. Dictionary for Social Professions. Deutsch – Englisch/Englisch – Deutsch. Mit elektronischem Wörterbuch und Trainingsprogramm/With Electronic Dictionary and Training Programme, Fachhochschule Frankfurt/M./University of Hull. Verf.: Wilhelm Kahl, Greta Bradley, Frankfurt/M.: Fachhochschulveralg, 1994
* Wörterbuch Soziale Arbeit. Bd. 1: Deutsch – Englisch. Englisch – Deutsch. Hrsg.: Deutscher Verein für öffentliche und private Fürsorge, Frankfurt/M., Red.: Manfred van der Mark. Frankfurt/M.: Deutscher Verein für öffentliche und private Fürsorge, 1988
* Fachlexikon der Sozialen Arbeit; Hrsg.: Deutscher Verein für öffentliche und private Fürsorge; Frankfurt/M.: Eigenverlag; 2002[5]
* European Communities: Glossary. Institutions, policies and enlargement of the European Union, Luxembourg: Office for official Publications of the European Communities, 2000
* Wates, Nick (compiler and editor): The Community Planning Handbook. How People can shape their cities, towns and villages in any part of the world. London: Earthscan Publications, 2000
* Bibliographisches Institut & F.A. Brockhaus AG, Langenscheidt KG: Duden – PC-Bibliothek 2.1 mit Plus-Paket. Revision 15, Dudenverlag, 1999

Danksagung

Mein Dank geht an viele Personen, die mir unmittelbar bei der Stichwörterauswahl geholfen haben und ebenso mir Anregungen für die Wahl der korrekten Übersetzung gaben – manchmal nur durch eine nebenbei gemachte Bemerkung. Freilich konnten Fehler oder Auslassungen nicht vollständig vermieden werden – und die Verantwortung hierfür liegt letztlich allein bei mir. Persönlich nennen möchte ich folgende Personen:

* Kusche, Christoph, Fachhochschule Nordost-Niedersachsen, Fachbereich Sozialwesen, Lüneburg
* Lange, Chris, Alice Salomon Schule, Berlin
* Leeson, Lorraine, Director of the Centre for Deaf Studies, Dublin
* Meade, Rosemary, Department of Applied Social Studies, University College of Cork
* O'Gready, Mary, Disability Support Office, University College of Cork
* Pfannendörfer, Gerhard, Redaktionsbüro der Zeitschriften Blätter der Wohlfahrtspflege, SOCIALmanagement und Sozialwirtschaft aktuell, Frankfurt/Main
* Scheipl, Josef, Universität Graz
* Schöttler, Gitta, Frankfurt am Main

Mein ganz besonderer Dank aber gilt Manfred Wolf vom Eigenverlag des Deutschen Vereins für öffentliche und private Fürsorge, Frankfurt/Main – ohne ihn wäre dies Projekt nicht zustande gekommen und es hätte auch nicht in dieser Weise realisiert werden können.

Introduction

Technicalities

🕮 cross reference to glossary

⇒ cross reference in the respective section, i.e. the German-English, the English-German or glossary section of the dictionary

The project

Even if this document is thought as dictionary in the traditional sense there is another purpose closely attached. We are presenting terms that showed as being specifically relevant for those concerned with social issues and their development. This is a revised version of the dictionary *Soziale Arbeit. Deutsch – English, English – Deutsch from 1988 (Hrsg.: Deutscher Verein für öffentliche und private Fürsorge, Frankfurt/M/. 1988).*

A first change is that we are not focussing solely on *Social Work* as the title suggests. Already in that edition, however, the term Social Work had been understood in a wider meaning. The fact is that the views of the different sub-disciplines are more and more blurred – thus, we are actually compiling a wide set of terms that are important for any work in the social area. However, neither completeness of the terms listed nor exclusiveness are claimed.

What can be found as translation of each term is not necessarily the complete list of meanings – for example: the term *atomised* had been translated as *vereinzelt, zersplittert,* it can mean as well *zertäubt,* a meaning that had not been listed as it does not specifically reflect the social dimension of the meaning, in which we are interested. Furthermore, here we are mainly dealing with different meanings of terms rather than with the linguistic side. This can mean that the translation of a term is listed as noun, but not the meaning of the term in its use as a verb (see e.g. drink).

Reworking the original document brought up many of the fascinating issues around language as a living medium, marked by an internal development but much more by the reflection of the social and societal changes. This goes as far as the listing of some terms only in the glossary as they are "newly created" and what is asked for had been not the translation but simply the introduction of the term. One example for this is the term *communitisation.*

What in general was of striking appearance was to consider systematically the terms that had been thought of as necessary to be added. These changes – additions and omissions – reflected very much the changes of social professional approaches and of institutional and statutory social challenges. Thus, a bulk of terms is pointing in one or another direction on terms of management, administering and not least on dealing with financial restrictions.

Another point in this connection is that some terms are obsolete, some are political incorrect or questionable – as we are all more or less aware the matter of political correctness is getting very much a concern of using language. In addition there is a grey area where terms had been getting contestable because of their use for something that is generally seen as reprehensible. Here the term *psychohygiene* is typical. *Psychohygiene* as real means of control and subordination had been widely misused during fascism. At the same time it is a term which still is used by the World Health Organisation, even if with a different meaning.

So, already the listing of terms has very much a paradigmatic dimension, as well, goes far beyond a simple translation or its interpretation.

As well, listing the terms had thoroughly to be considered. Even if several terms had been simply taken from other dictionaries, those existing documents had only been taken as stimulation. The other way round the aim of the current book is not to replace them – important terms had not been repeated here. The criteria of inclusion had been twofold, namely (a) mentioning reoccurring problems in translating specific terms (personally experienced or recognised through questions by others, on conferences etc.) and (b) looking for terms that had been only recently developed in their relevance in social science.

The translation, then, is in many cases very much depending on the school or approach behind it. This gets clear for example when we look at the different possible ways of translating Milieu as *Milieu (Umgebung), milieu, social environment, social setting* – actually, some other possibilities could be added. Sometimes, and as far as language is a creative activity it may be helpful in translations to look a term up in a thesaurus, but be aware that in many cases the meaning as it is suggested by the superficial impression can be misleading – the term *rehabilitation,* as it is used in various languages actually has in many cases a very different meaning when it comes to important details.

However, as ambitious all this sounds, the presented dictionary is in fact only a small tool that hopefully can provide some help for those working in any social area in both languages.

A further remark is important in regard of the "origin". In pragmatic terms the British-English spelling is used. But this has as well a substantial background despite the pragmatic dimension that in the EU British-English is more likely *the* language, which counts rather than American-English (this can be said without being a linguistic puritan). What actually is more important here is the fact that, speaking of terms of relevance in the social area British-English is of specific relevance in its determination of the subject. Without discussing this matter in detail we have to face the important role of the British tradition in its meaning for the development of social professions. This does not mean that other traditions are unimportant. To state this is only concerned with the fact that here in Europe it is the British tradition rather than the American we are dealing with. This is true even if processes of globalisation and already early international orientations of social professions looked well across the Atlantic.

The decision of which language to take as point of departure for this dictionary was in part – and in favour for taking the German as point of departure – set in advance by the original dictionary from 1988. However, the recent developments made it tempting to start from the English and revise the dictionary from this perspective. In substantial terms the reason for this is that there is a strong influence from here which brings to some extent different "subdisciplines" closer together. It is in particular the acknowledgement of the three main strands community work, social work and social policy as independent disciplines which actually allows – paradoxically – for more integration. In the German tradition, on the other hand, the subordination of community work approaches under social work (📖 social intervention) leads to a neglect of the meaning of each of the subjects, namely *Gemeinwesenarbeit* and *Sozialarbeit.* In this sense there is a well acknowledged meaning of a British social work tradition in Europe. Such a comment includes the interpretation that social work in the British tradition simply absorbed social pedagogies, a discipline that had and still has a rather strong independent position in the German context. This means as well, that it can be assumed that many of the users will see such a dictionary as a tool to support their own efforts to approach texts of English origin. Furthermore, expressing themselves in English happens in contexts where the (British) English is the point of reference (even though we have to face the fact that on these occasions the British-English is for many times more Pidgin-English than anything else).

Of course, we can not offer a language course. However, a single remark will be allowed. In German, it is a habit to combine words and construct mammoth. And a trend is to transfer this practice into English language. This is a very common practice in the area we are working in as we are dealing with complex settings, multidimensional aspects of social live etc., which, of course, suggest such "combinations". In fact, it is true, that such a trend is noticeable even amongst native English speakers. However, correct is to use a more verb oriented style, i.e. to "grasp and describe processes" rather than "stating structures". Thus, it would be more appropriate to use "reconciliation of (the) family, ~ of family members" rather than speak of "family reconciliation". However, in many of these cases it is a matter of personal taste and style, and as well a matter of academic style, traditions, regional orientation etc. Especially with the spread of Pidgin-English the trend of using nouns is on the increase. At the same time it makes some sense to consider, what had been said before: the use of verbs as the reflection of processes and the use of nouns as orientation on structures (and of course, this brings us to the fact that language is a process, and not just a communication which has a structure).

Sources

The references given in the following had been helpful tools to develop the list of terms and to reflect the translations.

* Halbach, Günter et altera: Labour Law in Germany: an overview, Ed.: Federal Ministry of Labour and Social Affairs, Bonn 1994[5]
* Bauer, Rudolph (Ed.): Lexikon des Sozial- und Gesundheitswesens, München/Wien: R. Oldenbourg Verlag, 1992
* Wörterbuch für Sozialberufe. Dictionary for Social Professions. Deutsch – Englisch/Englisch – Deutsch. Mit elektronischem Wörterbuch und Trainingsprogramm/With Electronic Dictionary and Training Programme, Fachhochschule Frankfurt/M./University of Hull. Verf.: Wilhelm Kahl, Greta Bradley, Frankfurt/M.: Fachhochschulverlag, 1994
* Wörterbuch Soziale Arbeit. Bd. 1: Deutsch – Englisch. Englisch – Deutsch. Hrsg.: Deutscher Verein für öffentliche und private Fürsorge, Frankfurt/M., Red.: Manfred van der Mark. Frankfurt/M.: Deutscher Verein für öffentliche und private Fürsorge, 1988
* Fachlexikon der Sozialen Arbeit; Hrsg.: Deutscher Verein für öffentliche und private Fürsorge; Frankfurt/M.: Eigenverlag; 2002[5]
* European Communities: Glossary. Institutions, policies and enlargement of the European Union, Luxembourg: Office for official Publications of the European Communities, 2000

* Wates, Nick (compiler and editor): The Community Planning Handbook. How People can shape their cities, towns and villages in any part of the world, London: Earthscan Publications, 2000
* Bibliographisches Institut & F.A. Brockhaus AG, Langenscheidt KG: Duden – PC-Bibliothek 2.1 mit Plus-Paket. Revision 15, Dudenverlag, 1999

Acknowledgements

My words of a special Thank You go to many people, helping immediately with drawing the list of terms and then the interpretation or just with reminding me by a quick hint what should be included. Of course, errors could not completely be avoided – and I take the responsibility for them. Being aware of this I want to name the following individuals:

* Kusche, Christoph, Fachhochschule Nordost-Niedersachsen, Fachbereich Sozialwesen, Lüneburg
* Lange, Chris, Alice Salomon Schule, Berlin
* Leeson, Lorraine, Director of the Centre for Deaf Studies, Dublin
* Meade, Rosemary, Department of Applied Social Studies, University College of Cork
* O'Gready, Mary, Disability Support Office, University College of Cork
* Pfannedörfer, Gerhard, Redaktionsbüro der Zeitschriften Blätter der Wohlfahrtspflege, SOCIALmanagement und Sozialwirtschaft aktuell, Frankfurt/Main
* Scheipl, Josef, Universität Graz
* Schöttler, Gitta, Frankfurt am Main

However, my very special words of Thank You go to Manfred Wolf, Eigenverlag, Deutscher Verein für öffentliche und private Fürsorge, Frankfurt/M. – Without his engagement this project would not have come to existence; and it would have not been realised in such a pleasant and supportive atmosphere.

DEUTSCH – ENGLISCH/ GERMAN – ENGLISH

– A –

Abbau (Arbeitskräfte, Leistungen) reduction, curtailment – (med.) decline, decay, (psych.) (mental) decline

abbrechen (Studium etc.) to drop out

Abendschule evening school, evening class

Abenteuerspielplatz adventure playground

Aberglaube superstition

aberkennen to deprive sb. of sth., disallow, to declare sb. disentitled

aberkennen der bürgerlichen Rechte to deprive sb. of civil rights

Abfall refuse

Abfindung (bei Beendigung eines Arbeitsverhältnisses) redundancy payment, compensation, (jur.) settlement

Abgabe ⇒ Steuer

Abhängigkeit (von Personen, Drogen) dependency

Abkommen agreement

ablehnen refuse

Ablehnung rejection, refusal

Ablehnungsbescheid notice of rejection, refusal

ablösen (neues Gesetz das frühere) supersede, replace

Ablösungsprozess (psych.) process of detachment

Abmachung agreement, arrangement

Abmeldung notice of change of situation (address etc.)

abschieben deport

Abschiebung (Ausländer) deportation (of foreigners, of non-nationals) summary return to country of origin

Absicherung (Anspruch) safeguard

Abschlusszeugnis leaving cert

Abstammung descending, family origin

Absteiger, sozialer sb. losing status, moving down the social scale

abstimmen vote, coordinate

Abstimmung (über einen Fall) ⇒ Angleichung

Abstimmung zwischen Trägern coordination

Abstinenz (Alkohol, Drogen) abstinence

Abstinenzler teetotaller, total abstainer

abstreiten deny

Abstrich (bei Forderungen) concession

Abstrich (bei Leistungen) cut, reduction, curtailment

Abstrich (med.) smear, swab

Abstufung gradation

Abtreibung ⇒ Schwangerschaftsabbruch

abtreten (Forderung) assign, cede (claim)

Abtretung (jur.) assignment, cession

Abwägung consideration of pros and cons

Abwägung aller Umstände weighing all the circumstances, balancing

Abwägung, unter Abwägung on balance

Abwehrmechanismus mechanism of defence

abweichendes Verhalten deviant behaviour, deviance

Abweichung deviance, anomie

Abwertung (psych.) disparagement, depreciation

Abwesenheit absenteeism

Abwesenheitspflegschaft curator for an absent person, curator absentis (USA)

abzahlen pay off

Abzahlung payment by instalments

Abzahlungsvertrag hire purchase contract

Abzug deduction

abzugsfähig deductable

Adoleszenz adolescence

Adoption (-sbeschluss) adoption (order)

Adoptionshilfe aid with adoption, support of adoption support

Adoptiveltern adoptive parents, missverstanden teils auch foster parents (dies bezieht sich auf vorübergehende Pflegeelternschaft)

Adoptivkind adopted child, foster child (*foster parents/ children* bezieht sich im Deutschen streng genommen auf den Pflegebegriff, ist juristisch also nicht unbedingt mit einer Adoption verbunden)

Äquivalenzprinzip principle of equivalence

Ärger trouble, hassle

ärztliche Dienste (soz.) medical services

ärztliche Krankenpflege (medical) nursing

ärztliche Untersuchung medical examination

ärztliche Versorgung medical care, medical treatment

ärztliche Versorgung (soz.) medical care

Affekt emotion, affect, uncontrolled behaviour

Agentur agency
🕮 Wohlfahrtsverband

Aggression aggression

Aggressionsverhalten aggressive behaviour

Aggressivität aggressiveness

agieren act, (psych.) acting out

AIDS (erworbene Immunschwächekrankheit) Acquired Immune Deficiency Syndrome

Akkulturation acculturation, cultural integration

Akte file, record, dossier

Aktenanalyse (für Forschungszwecke) file analysis, document analysis

Akteneinsicht (Recht auf) inspection of records (right to), freedom of information

Aktenführung file-keeping

Aktenstudium examination of files

aktivierende Pflege activating care

Aktivierung activation

Aktivitätstheorie (sen.) activity theory

Aktivitätstherapie (sen.) activity therapy

Akzeptanz acceptance

Alimente maintenance payment (UK), support (USA)

Alkoholabhängigkeit alcohol dependency

Alkoholiker alcoholic

Alkohilismus alcoholism

Alkoholmissbrauch alcohol abuse

allein erziehende Mutter und Vater ⇒ Einelternfamilie

allein stehend single, unmarried, unattached

Allgemeinbildung general education

Allgemeininteresse public interest

Allgemeinwohl public weal, common weal

Allgemeine Ortskrankenkasse (AOK) local health insurance (fund)

Allgemeiner Sozialdienst (ASD) general social service, frequently: one-stop shop

Altenbegegnungsstätte day-center for senior citizens
📖 elderly

Altenbeirat senior citizen advisory board

Altenberatung counselling for the aged, advice for senior citizens (der Begriff des *counselling* weist eine große Nähe zu psychologischer Beratung/Therapie auf)

Altenbildung adult education for the elderly, education for senior citizens, education for the Third Age

Altendienste services for the services for senior citizens

Alteneinrichtungen residential (institutional) care for the elderly, nursing homes

Altenerholung holidays for the elderly

Altengymnastik gymnastics for the elderly

Altenheim (Altersheim, Seniorenheim) residential home for the aged, old people's home, nursing home

Altenhilfe special support for the elderly

Altenplanung planning for the elderly

Altenklub older persons' club

Altenkrankenheim (Altenpflegeheim) nursing home for the elderly

Altenkrankenpflege geriatric nursing

Altenpflege care of the elderly

Altenpflegehelfer/in geriatric nursing assistant

Altenpfleger/in geriatric nurse

Altenpflegekräfte personal assistant for older person, age care people

Altensport sports for the elderly

Altentagesstätte day centre for senior citizens with nursing and day hospital

Altenwohnanlage purpose-built housing for the elderly

Altenwohnheim sheltered housing (service flats) for the elderly

Altenwohnung special flats for the elderly

Altern (Substatntiv und Verb) (biographisch, demographisch) aging

Altern (Substatntiv und Verb) (biol., med.) senescence

Alterspsychologie gerontopsychology, psychology of aging

Altersaufbau (einer Bevölkerung) (stat.) (population's) age structure

Altersforschung gerontology

Altersgrenze age limit

Altersgruppe age group; (Statistik) cohort

Altershilfe für Landwirte ⇒ landwirtschaftliche Alterskassen

Alterskrankheiten, Lehre von den geriatrics

Alterspsychiatrie gerontopsychiatry, psychogeriatrics

Altersruhegeld (Altersrente, Pension) old age pension, retirement pension

Altersruhegeld, flexibles flexible pension

Altersruhegeld, vorgezogenes premature pension

Altersruhegeld, vorzeitiges (i.w.S.) early retirement pension

Altersschwäche senility, decrepitude

Alterssicherung (finanziell) financial security for old age

Alterssicherung provisions for old age (dies kann zu Missverständnissen führen, da *provisions for old age* auch die Bedeutung der *Altersvorsorge* annehmen kann)

Alterssoziologie gerontosociology, sociology of aging

Altersversorgung, betriebliche old age pension from the company, enterprise pension scheme

Altstadtsanierung urban redevelopment, regeneration

Alzheimersche Krankheit Alzheimer's disease

ambulante ärztliche Behandlung out-patient medical treatment/out-patient care

Ambulanz out-patient ward, ambulance (Transport)

Amt office, function, agency

Amt antreten take up office

Amt ausüben being in office

Amt, vom Amt zurücktreten resign

amtlich official

Amt, von Amts wegen ex officio, officially

Amtsarzt medical officer of health, medical referee (USA)

amtsärztliches Gutachten medical report, medical certificate

Amtseid official oath, oath of office (USA)

Amtseid ablegen to take the official oath

Amtsermittlung official investigation

Amtsgeheimnis official secret

Amtsgericht local court

Amtsgewalt official authority

Amtshaftung liability of an official

Amtshilfe, Ersuchen um request for administrative or legal assistance

Amtsmissbrauch abuse of (official) authority malfeasance

Amtsmündel ward of court

Amtspflegschaft official curatorship, trusteeship

Amtsvormund official guardian

Amtsvormundschaft statutory (public) guardianship

Anamnese medical, social history

Anerkennung (Anspruch, Examen) acknowledgement recognition

Anfall (med.) seizure, attack, fit, paroxysm, spasm

Anfechtung (jur.) challenging

Anfechtung der Anerkennung der Vaterschaft paternity suit

Anfang start, beginning

Anfang, von Anfang an, von Neuem beginnen from the scratch

Anfechten contest, contestation, challenge, question

Anfrage request

angeboren (z.B. Behinderung) congenital, innate

Angebot offer, provision

Angebot (soz., päd.) available capacities, offer

Angehörige(r) relative, kin

angemessen reasonable, appropriate, adequate

angemessene Strafe just punishment

Angepasstheit conformity, being adapted

Angestellte(r) salaried worker

Angestelltenrentenversicherung Salaried Employees' Pension Insurance (Social Security for white collar employees)

Angleichung adjustment, harmonisation

Angleichung (Gesetze, Maßnahmen) mutual adjustment

Angriff raid

Angst fear (psych.) anxiety

Anhörung Beteiligter hearing of the parties involved

Anhörungsverfahren hearing procedure

Anklage charge, indictment, accusation

anklagen (v., jur.) charge, accuse, indict (USA), blame (eher anschuldigen, nicht jur.)

Anlage (biol.) hereditary trait

Anlage (psych., päd.) trait, predisposition

Anlage und Umwelt nature and nurture

Anleitung (von Mitarbeitern) supervision, briefing

Anliegerstaat bordering country

Anmeldung registration

Annahme (psych.) acceptance, assumption, presumption, presupposition

Annahme als Kind adoption

annulieren annul

anomal, **anormal** anomalous, abnormal, anormal (USA)

Anordnung arrangement, composition

Anpassung adaption, adjustment, accommodation

Anpassungsfähigkeit adaptability

anrechnen (v.) (in Ansatz bringen) reckon, calculate, setting off

anrechnungsfähig (i.S.v. absetzbar) deductible

anrechnungsfähig (Jahre) countable (years), reckonable

anrechnungspflichtig, reckonable

Anschubfinanzierung seed capital

Anspruch claim

Anspruch erheben claim

Anspruch im Ausland (z.B.Rente) (s.S.) entitlement abroad (e.g. pension)

Anspruch, übertragbarer Anspruch alienable or transferable claim

anspruchsberechtigt eligble, entitled to claim

Anspruchsniveau (psych.) level of aspiration, pretensions

Anstalt institution, establishment (UK)

Anstalt, geschlossene closed institution

Anstalt, offene open institution

Anstaltseinweisung institutionalisation, admission to an institution

Anstaltseinweisung, erneuerte Anstaltseinweisung, Wiedereinweisung re-institutionalisation, readmission to an institution

Anstaltshilfe assistance-workerin an institution

Anteilnahme interest, participation, (Mitgefuehl) sympathy

Antrag (adm.) application

Antragsberechtigung entitlement to apply

Antragsteller applicant

antreten (Amt) entering (into) office, taking office

antreten (Beweis) offer proof, evidence, giving evidence

antreten (Strafe) begin to serve a sentence

Anwartschaft(srecht) expectant (right)

Anwartschaftszeit qualifying period

Anzeige (Benachrichtigung) noticfication, information

Anzeige (Straftat) complaint, report

Anzeige erstatten notice

anzeigen, (jemanden) to report (sb.) to the police

anzweifeln doubt, question, contest

arbeiten work, (in Ausnahmefällen) labour

Arbeit labour (als Tätigkeit), work (als Erwerbstätigkeit, aber eher mit konkretem Tätigkeitsbezug), employment (Erwerbstätigkeit)

Arbeiter/in, angelernte semiskilled worker

Arbeiter, ausländische foreign workers, migrant workers

Arbeiter, gelernte (Facharbeiter) skilled workers

Arbeiter, illegale ausländische Arbeiter illegal immigrant workers

Arbeiterbildung workers' education

Arbeiterkolonie workers' settlement

Arbeiterrentenversicherung Wage-Earners' Pension Insurance (Social security for workers), insurance authority for (manual) workers

Arbeitnehmerfreibetrag (Steuer) (D) income deductible (for employees)

Arbeitnehmersparzulage employee saving bonus

Arbeitsamt (local) employment (labour) office, job centre

Arbeitsaufnahmeförderung help starting work

Arbeitsbedingungen working conditions

Arbeitsbeschaffung (allgemeine Maßnahme zur Förderung der Beschäftigung) job creation (general measure for the promotion of employment)

Arbeitserlaubnis labour permit

Arbeitserprobung (Behinderter) work test

Arbeitsfähigkeit ability to work

Arbeitsgemeinschaft (i.e.S.) working group, study team

Arbeitsgruppe working party

Arbeitshaus work house

Arbeitshilfen, technische (Behinderte) (technical) aids for work

Arbeitskraft (Leistungsvermögen) capacity to work

Arbeitssicherheit safety at work

Arbeitssuchende/r job seeker

Arbeitsteilung (gesellschaftliche) division of labour, (individuell, arbeitsplatzbezogen) job sharing

Arbeitsunfall occupational accidence

Arbeitsverfassung works constitution

Arbeitsvertrag employment contract

arbeitslos (gemeldet) ⇒ erwerbslos unemployed (registered as), out-of-work, jobless, redundant, erwerbslos, vorübergehend (temporarily) laid-off

Arbeitslosengeld (D) unemployment benefit, job seekers allowance (UK), compensation (USA)

Arbeitslosenhilfe (D) unemployment relief (or assistance)

Arbeitslosenkrankenversicherung health insurance for the unemployed

Arbeitslosenquote unemployment rate

Arbeitslosenversicherung unemployment insurance

Arbeitslosenzahl number of unemployed

Arbeitslosigkeit unemployment

Arbeitslosigkeit, amtlich erfasste official unemployment

Arbeitslosigkeit, kurzfristige short term unemployment

Arbeitslosigkeit, langfristige long term unemployment

Arbeitsmarkt labour market

Arbeitsmarktlage situation on the labour market

Arbeitsmedizin occupational health care

Arbeitspflicht duty to work

Arbeitsplatz work place

Arbeitsplatzerhaltung job protection

Arbeitsplatzteilung job sharing, division

arbeitsscheu work-shy

Arbeitsschutz safety at work

Arbeits- und Beschäftigungstherapie occupational therapy

Arbeitsunfähigkeit disability to work

Arbeitsunfall accident at work, industrial, occupational accident

Arbeitsvermittlung labour exchange, employment service, employment agency, job placement office, Employment Office, jobcentre (UK)

Arbeitsvertrag work contract, contract of employment

Arbeitsverwaltung labour administration

Arbeitsverweigerung refusal to work

arbeitswillig willing (or ready) to work

Armenrecht ⇒ Prozesskostenhilfe

Armut poverty

Armut, äußerste ~ destitution, immiseration

Armut über Generationen, andauernde Armut pauperism, cycle of deprivation (obsolete as term here, today the term would be used to describe multidimensionality of poverty

Armutsgrenze poverty line

Armutsfalle poverty trap (UK), poverty plateau (USA)

Arzneimittelabhängigkeit drug dependency

Arzneimissbrauch drug abuse

Arzneisucht drug addiction

Arzt/Ärztin physician, medical doctor

Arzt/ Ärztin für Gemeinmedizin general practitioner

Arztgeheimnis medical secret

Arztwahl, freie free choice of doctor

asozial (abwertend) asocial, dissocial, anti-social

Asyl (jur.) asylum

Asyl (Zufluchtsort) refuge, sanctuary

asylberechtigt entitled to granted asylum

Asylbewerber applicant for asylum, asylum seeker

Asylrecht asylum law, right of asylum

Attest medical certificate

aufeinander folgend successive

Aufenthalt abode

Aufenthalt, derzeitiger Aufenthalt present abode, current address

Aufenthalt, fester Aufenthalt domicile

Aufenthalt, gewöhnlicher Aufenthalt ordinary, (or habitual) residence, habitual abode

Aufenthaltsberechtigung right, entitlement of residence

Aufenthaltsbestimmung (Elternrecht) decision on (or control of) domicile

Aufenthaltserlaubnis residence permit

Aufenthaltserlaubnis, befristete (time-)limited residence permit

Aufenthaltserlaubnis, unbefristete unlimited residence permit

Aufgabenbereich scope of duty, tasks

Aufgabenübertragung transfer of tasks, delegation

Aufhebung (jur.) repeal, abolition, (doppelte Bedeutung von Aufhebung als Überwindung und Bewahrung, Dialektik der Aufhebung) sublation and supersession

Aufhebungsmitteilung delivery of notice of termination

Auflage (Weisung) condition, direction

Aufnahmegruppe receiving group

Aufnahmestation (med.) admission ward

Aufschub postponement (Eingriff, Zahlung) delay, respite

Aufsichtsbehörde (Versicherungsaufsichtsamt usw.) inspectorate (of insurance sector, of social services, of prisons, of education etc.) (UK)

Aufsichtspflicht (Eltern) (jur.) (parental) duty (parental) of supervision, duty of parents of supervision/to supervise

aufsteigen, sozial to be upwardly mobile

aufstockende Leistung additional allowance, supplementary benefit

Aufstockung (s.S.) increase of benefits, additional payment

aufsuchende Sozialarbeit (Straßensozialarbeit, Hausbesuche bzw. Angebot von Besuch ohne Anforderung) outreach (social) work

Aufwandsentschädigung reimbursement (of expenses)

Aufwertung revaluation

Ausbildung (i.w.S.) training, education

Ausbildung, berufsbegleitende employment based education, sandwich courses

Ausbildung, betriebliche on-the-job training

Ausbildung, schulische school based education

Ausbildung, überbetriebliche joint vocational training

Ausbildungsplatz apprenticeship

Ausbildungsförderung promotion of education (or training), system of educational grants, scholarships

Ausbildungshilfe educational assistance, training benefits

ausbrechen escape, break out

Auseinandersetzung hassle

Ausfallbürge deficiency guarantor

Ausfall- und Ersatzzeiten (s.S.) (D) excluded, non-payment periods in old age pension insurance (e.g. on grounds of unemployment or military service), which are nevertheless counted towards the pension

Ausführungsbestimmung implementing regulation, implementing order

Ausgleichsabgabe (Schwerbehindertengesetz) (D) equalization levy (because of failure to employ the necessary percentage of disabled persons)

Ausgleichszahlung compensation (payment)

ausgrenzen (soziol.) marginalise, (nicht festgelegt von/in welchem Bereich) exclude

Ausgrenzung marginalisation, exclusion

Auskunftsverweigerungsrecht (bei Gefahr eigener strafrechtlicher Verfolgung) right to withhold information

Ausländer/in foreigner, stranger, alien 🕮 Ausländer

Ausländerfeindlichkeit hostility to foreigners, xenophobia

Ausländerpolitik policy concerning foreigners (sometimes used: aliens), immigration policy

Ausländerrecht law concerning foreign nationals

Ausländersozialarbeit social work with (social services to) foreigners, immigrants, exiles

Auslieferung (politisch, juristisch) extradition, (Lieferung) delivery

aussondern section-off

Ausreißer/in run-away

Ausrichtung bias

Aussage statement

Aussage, schriftliche (jur.) affidavit

Aussage, mündliche (jur.) evidence, testimony

Aussage, schriftliche oder unterschriebene deposition

Aussagegenehmigung permission to give evidence

Aussageverweigerungsrecht ⇒ Zeugnisverweigerungsrecht

Ausschreibung invitation to bid, ⇒ Stellenausschreibung

Ausschuss committee, commission, board (auch als Vorstand)

Außendienst outreach

Außendienstfürsorge für psychisch Kranke community care for the mentally ill

Außendienststelle area office, branch office

außerehelich (Beziehung ⇒ nichtehelich) extra marital (relationship)

außergerichtlich extrajudicial

außerschulische Bildung extra-curricular education

Aussiedler/in resettlers, repatriate

Aussiedlerhilfe resettlement aid

Aussteiger/in dropout

Ausweis (Personal-) identity card (proof of identity)

Ausweisung (jur.) expulsion, deportation

Auswirkung impact, spill-over, effect, repercussion

Auszubildende/r apprentice, trainee

– B –

Bagatellbetrag negligible amount

Bagatelldelikt minor offence

Bagatellsachen minor cases

Bahnhofsmission Travellers' Aid Society, passenger aid, passenger aid on the railway station 📖 traveller

Ballungsgebiet agglomeration, area of agglomeration

Barbetrag ⇒ Taschengeld

Barmherzigkeit mercy, charity

Basisarbeit work at the basis, work at the grassroots

baufällig derelict

Baukostenzuschuss brick and mortar subsidy

Bausparkasse building society

Beamte/r/~in civil servant, official, (public) officer

Beamtenversorgung civil servants pension

Beauftragte/r commissioner

Beauftragte/r, Ausländer~ commissioner for foreign nationals

Beauftragte/r, Behinderten~ commissioner for peoples with disabilities (~ for the disabled/ disabled people, the handicapped

Beauftragte/r, Datenschutz~ commissioner for data protection

Beauftragte/r, Frauen~ commissioner for women's affairs

Beauftragte/r, Jugendmedienschutz~ commissioner for the legal protection of youth in respect to the media

Beauftragte/r, Kinderschutz~ commissioner for the protection of children, child protection

Bebauungsplan (adm.) (urban) development plan, land utilisation plan

Bedarf (Bedürfnis) requirement, need, (Nachfrage) demand, want

Bedarfsanalyse analysis of demand

Bedarfsdeckungsprinzip principle in the law of social assistance, that only the (minimum) requirements are covered

Bedarfsermittlung (Sozialplanung) need(s) assessment, ascertainment of need

Bedarfsgemeinschaft requirements of persons (family) living in the same household

Bedarfsmengenschema pattern of need

Bedarfsplanung demand planning

Bedürfnis need, want

bedürftig in need of sth. needy

Bedürftigkeit neediness, indigence

Bedürftigkeitsprüfung (soz.) means, income test

befähigen (v., soz.) enable, empower

Befähigung (Arbeit) competence, qualification (job)

Befähigung (Gemeinwesenarbeit) enablement, empowerment

Beförderung transport

Beförderung, unentgeltliche für Schwerbehinderte free travel for severely handicapped

Beförderung, unentgeltliche für Schüler free school transport

Beförderung (dienstl., teils auch i.S.v. befähigen) promotion

Beförderungsdienste transport facilities

Beförderungszuschuss (soz.) mobility allowance

Befragung survey, inquiry

Befreiung (Verpflichtung, Steuern) exemption

Befugnis entitlement, authority

Befugnis (jur.) competence

Befund (med., soz.) finding, result

Befund, ohne (generell) normal, negative result

Befund, ohne (o.B.) (med.) no appreciable disease (n.a.d.)

Befund, ohne (psych.) no abnormality discernible (n.a.d.)

Befürwortung recommendation, support

Begabtenförderung promotion of gifted children, students

Beglaubigung (jur.) authentication

Begleitdienst (soz.) accompanying service

begleitend (Maßnahme) concomitant, accompanying (measure), supplementing measure

begleitend (Studie) monitoring (study)

Begleitung guidance, company

Begutachtung expert opinion, assessment, certification

Behandlung (eines Vorganges) handling

Behandlung, ärztliche medical treatment

Behandlungspflege therapeutic nursing

Behandlungspflegschaft curatorship for a person under treatment

behindern impede

behindert disabled, handicapped impaired, having special needs

Behinderte/r people/person with special needs (disabled, handicapped people)

Behindertenberatung counselling for people with special needs (handicapped people), advising people with special needs (handicapped people)

Behinderteneinrichtung service for people with special needs

behindertengerecht accessible for people with disabilities

Behindertenhilfe disability allowance, not yet common: allowance for people with special needs

Behindertenhilfeplanung planning services for people with special needs (handicapped people)

Behindertenklubs clubs for people with special needs (handicapped people)

Behindertenpädagogik pedagogics for people with special needs

Behindertensport sports of people with special needs (handicapped people)

Behindertenverbände associations of people with special needs (handicapped people)

Behindertenwerkstatt ⇒ Werkstatt für Behinderte

Behindertenwohnheim home, hostel for disabled people (independent living, supervised or sheltered)

Behinderung disability, handicap

Behörde public authority, office

Beihilfe (financial) aid, allowance, assistance, grant, subsidy

Beihilfe zu einer Straftat aiding and abetting, being an accomplice

Beihilfe, einmalige (in Verbindung mit laufenden Zahlungen) (soz.) allowances for specific purposes (e.g. to buy clothing), discretionary allowances

Beirat board (beratend: advisory, wissenschaftlich: scientific)

Beistand (jur.) legal counsel

Beistand für die Ausübung der elterlichen Sorge guardian to assist the parent, who had the parental care

Beitrag (s.S.) contribution, social tax (USA)

Beitragsbemessungsgrenze (s.S.) income limit for the assessment of contributions

beitragsfrei non-contributory

beitragspflichtig (beitragsgebunden) contributory

Beitragszeit contribution period

Bekleidungshilfe clothing allowance

belastend (jur.) incriminating

belastend (psych.) taxing, distressing

Belästigung (insbes. von Frauen, Kindern) molestation, harrassement

Belästigung, sexuelle sexual harassment

Belastungserprobung (Behinderte) test of strength

Beleidigung insult

Belohnung award

Bemessungsgrundlage (s.S.) (pension) assessment basis

Bemessungsgrundlage, allgemeine (s.S.) general assessment basis

Bemessungsgrundlage, persönliche (s.S.) individual assessment basis

bemühen, sich bemühen um to strive for

benachteiligt disadvantaged, excluded, deprived

Benachteiligung (soz.) disadvantage, discrimination, deprivation

Benachteiligungssverbot (Frauen, Minderheiten) (jur.) legal ban on discrimination, legal prohibition of discrimination

Beobachtung observation, (evaluation, investigation)

Beobachtungsheim diagnostic assessment home, diagnostic observation home

Berater (jur.) advisor, (legal) counsel

Berater (psych.) counseller

Berater (med.) consultant

Beratung (jur.) legal advice

Beratung (allg.) advising

Beratung (med) consultation

Beratung (pol-administrativ, fin.) consulting

Beratung (soz., päd., jun., psych.) counselling

Berechtigung right, entitlement

Bereitschaftsdienst on-call, emergency service

Beruf occupation, vocation

berufliche Bildung vocational training

berufliche Rehabilitation vocational rehabilitation

berufliche Sozialisation vocational socialization

Berufsberatung vocational guidance, career counselling

Berufsbildungsbeihilfe vocational training allowance (federal)

Berufsausbildungsförderung promotion of vocational training

Berufsbildungswerk vocational training institute

Berufsfindung career, job search

Berufsfindungsjahr work experience year

berufsfördernde Rehabilitationsmaßnahmen measures for vocational rehabilitation

Berufsförderungswerk institute for the promotion of vocational training, institute promoting vocational training

Berufsgeheimnis professional secret, confidentiality

Berufsgenossenschaft (s.S.) (D) employers liability insurance association

Berufsgrundbildungsjahr (päd.) (year of) basic vocational training

Berufshilfen career assistance

Berufskrankheit occupational disease

Berufsorientierungsjahr ⇒ Berufsgrundbildungsjahr, Berufsfindungsjahr

Berufspraktikum ⇒ Praktikum

Berufsreife maturity for working life

Berufsschadensausgleich (Kriegsopfer) (D) compenasation for loss of income through war injury

Berufsunfähigkeit occupational disability

Berufsunfähigkeitsrente occupational disability pension

Berufsverband professional association

Berufsvorbereitung preparation for working life

Berufswahl, freie free choice of occupation

Berufswechsel change of occupation

Berufung (adm.) appointment, call

Berufung (jur.) appeal

Beschädigtenrente (vor allem an Kriegbeschädigte) (D) disability allowance, pension (esp. war injured)

Beschäftigung occupation, job

Beschäftigung, Haupt~ primary job, main job

Beschäftigung, Neben~ secondary job, sideline job

Beschäftigungsfähigkeit employability

Beschäftigungs- und Ausbildungsprogramme employment and training programmes

Beschäftigungsinitiativen locale initiatives to foster employment, (Existenzgründungs- und Trainingsprogramme der OECD) Initiatives for Local Employment Creation (ILE) and Enterprise Allowance Scheme of the OECD

Beschäftigungspflicht (der Arbeitgeber von Behinderten) duty to employ (disabled people in businesses)

Beschäftigungstherapie (psych.) occupational, work therapy

Bescheid (adm.) (official) notification

beschönigen gloss over

beschützende Arbeitsplätze sheltered work places

beschützende Werkstatt ⇒ Werkstatt für Behinderte

Beschwerde complaint, (juristische Anschuldigung) accusation

Besinnungslosigkeit senselessness, being out of control, (med.) consciousnesses, being without conscious

Besitzende und Besitzlose have and have-nots

Besitzer/in owner

Bessergestellte the well-to-do, better-off

Besserung (als Strafzweck) re-education, re-socialisation

Besserungsanstalt (veraltet) house of correction (obsolete)

Besserverdienende the better paid

Bestechung bribery

Bestimmung (adm.) provision

Bestrafung punishment, (jur.) penalty

Besuchsdienst (Freiwillige im Krankenhaus, Nachbarschaftshilfe) voluntary visiting

Besuchsrecht (geschiedener Eltern) (jur.) right of access

Betäubungsmittel narcotic (drug), anaesthetic

betreutes Wohnen sheltered, supervised housing, warden schemes

Betreuung care, attendance

Betreuung in der Wohnung (zu Hause) domiciliary care, services, in-home care (USA)

Betreuungsleistung care delivery

Betreuungsweisung (jur.) ⇒ Weisung

Betrieb company, (occasionally: firm), business

betriebliche Altersversorgung (zusätzliche Betriebsrente) (D) occupational pension scheme

betriebliche Gesundheitsfürsorge industrial, occupational medical service, occupational health provision, company health care

betriebliche Sozialarbeit occupational social work

betriebliche Sozialbetreuung company welfare services

betriebliche Sozialleistungen occupational welfare provisions

Betriebsarzt company doctor

Betriebskrankenkasse company based health insurance

Betriebsrat works council

Betriebsverfassung works constitution (concerning employees' rights of participation and complaint)

Betroffene people concerned

Betroffenenbeteiligung involvement (participation) of the people affected

Betroffenheit (Einfühlung) empathy

Betrug fraud, (Schummeln) cheating

betrügerisch fraudulent

betteln begging

Bettler/in beggar

Bettnässen bed-wetting, enuresis

Beunruhigung trouble

Beurkundung recording, certification, authentication

Beurteilung (päd.) appraisal, opinion

Beurteilung (Personalakte) report, personal file

Beurteilungsspielraum scope for assessment, judgement

Bevölkerungsabnahme (stat.) population decrease, decline

Bevölkerungsentwicklung (stat.) population development

Bevölkerungslehre demography

Bevölkerungspolitik population policy

Bevölkerungspyramide (stat.) age structure pyramid

Bevölkerungszunahme (stat.) population increase

Bewährung (jur.) probation

Bewährungsaufsicht supervision in probation

Bewährungshelfer probation officer

Bewährungshilfe probation service

Bewährungsfrist probation period

Bewährungsstrafe suspended sentence

Bewegung (soziol.) movement (political or social)

Bewegung an der Basis grass roots initiative (or movement)

Bewegungstherapie (med., sen.) physiotherapy, therapeutic gymnastics

Beweis proof, evidence

Beweislast burden of proof

Bewertung (bewertende Erfassung von Fakten, auch soziale Diagnose) assessment, diagnosis

Bewertung (Leistung, Ergebnis) (bes. päd.) appraisal

Bewertungsmethoden methods of evaluation

Bewusstsein consciousness, awareness

Bewusstseinserweiterung (psych.) enhancement, enlargement of consciousness

Bewusstseinsinhalt (psych.) conscious content

Bewusstseinslücke (psych.) amnesia

Bewusstseinsstörung mental disturbance, defective mental condition

Beziehungsgeflecht (soziol.) social network

Beziehungsgestaltung formation of relationship

Bezirkssozialarbeit area based social work

Bezug, räumlicher (Sozialplanung) relating to space

Bezugsgruppe (soziol.) reference group

Bezugsperson (päd., psych.) significant person

Bezugssystem reference system

bikulturelle Erziehung bicultural upbringing (and education)

Bildung education

Bildung, außerschulische extra-curricular education

Bildungsförderung promotion of education

Bildungsgesamtplan (D) overall plan for education

Bildungspolitik education policy

Bildungsreform educational reform

Bildungsurlaub study leave, educational leave

Bindung (jur.) obligation

Bindung (psych.) bonding

bindungslos unattached, foot-loose

Binnenwanderung internal migration

BIP (Bruttoinlandsprodukt) GDP (Gross Domestic Product)

Blinde blind people, the blind, (Sehbehinderte einschließlich Blinde) visually impaired (people)

Blindengeld blind allowance

Blindenhund guide dog (UK), seeing-eye dog (USA)

Blindenschrift Braille

Blindenware goods (articles) made by blind people

Blindenwerkstätte workshop for the blind

Bordell brothel

Brennpunkt, sozialer problem area, socially deprived area

Bruttoeinkommen gross income

BSP (Bruttosozialprodukt) GNP (gross national product

Bürde lot

Bügerinitiative community action group

Bundesangestelltentarifvertrag (BAT) collective agreement for federal employees

Bundesjugendplan (D) Federal Youth Plan

Bürge (jur.) guarantor

Bürgerangelegenheiten citizen affairs

Bürgerberatungsstelle Citizens Advice Bureau (UK)

Bürgerbeteiligung citizens' participation

Bürgerhaus civic centre

Bürgerinitiative citizens' initiative

Bürgernähe (soz., adm.) proximity to citizens

Bürgschaft guarantee

– C –

Chancengleichheit equal opportunities

Charakterbeurteilung assessment of character

charakterisieren characterise

Chauvinismus chauvinism

– D –

Dachorganisation umbrella-oraganisation

Darlehen loan

Daseinsvorsorge services of general interest (totality of) services for the public
🕮 Daseinsvorsorge

Datenanalyse data analysis

Datenschutz data protection

Datenschutzbeauftragter ⇒ Beauftragter

Datenverarbeitung, elektronische electronic data processing

Dauerarbeitsverhältnis permanent employment

Dauerbefürsorgte (A) permanent welfare recipients

Dauerpflege (~fall) (med.) (person requiring) permanent nursing, person requiring full-time care

Deliktfähigkeit responsibility for torts

Demenz dementia

Depression (psych.) depression

Depression, anhaltende ~ persistent depression

Deprivation deprivation

determinieren pre-empt

Deutung interpretation

Deutungsmuster pattern of interpretation

Devianz ⇒ Abweichung

Diagnose (med.) diagnosis

Diagnose (soz.) assessment, diagnosis

Dienst, sozialer social service

Dienstanweisung (adm.) instruction

Dienstaufsicht (adm.) administrative supervision, administrative control

Dienstaufsichtsbeschwerde complaint to official in charge

Dienstbefreiung (adm.) time off

dienstbereit on call

Dienstbereitschaft on duty

Dienstgeheimis official secret

Dienstunfähigkeit invalidity, disability for service

Dienstvertrag contract of employment

Diplom diploma

Drehtürpsychiatrie revolving door psychiatry

Drogen drugs, dope, "substances"

Drogenabhängigkeit drug dependency

Drogenberatung drug counselling

Drogenberatungsstelle drug counselling

Drogenberatungsstelle drug counselling centre

Drogenentwöhnung drug treatment

Drogenentzug drug withdrawal

Drogenhandel drug traffic

Drogenhändler pusher, dealer

Drogenhilfe aid with drug problems

Drogenkonsum drug taking

Drogenkonsument drug taker

Drogenmissbrauch (mehrfacher) drug abuse (multiple)

Drogenmissbrauchsbekämpfung drug control

Drogensucht drug addiction

Drogentherapie durg therapy

duales Ausbildungssystem dual training system

dürftig miserable, meagre

Durchführungsbestimmungen implementing regulations, statutory instruments

durchführbar viable, feasable

Durchführbarkeit (i.S. des sich lohnens) feasibility

Durchführbarkeit (techn.) feasibility

durchgehende Hilfe (durch Pflege) continuity of care

durchgehende Hilfe (sen.) continuous care

durchgehende Hilfe (Strafvollzug) continuous support

Durchsuchung (jur.) search

– E –

Eckregelsatz (soz.) (D) basic standard rates (social assistance)

Eckwert guiding value (nicht im Sinne des finanztechnischen Begriffs)

Ehe marriage

eheähnliche Gemeinschaft cohabitation

Eheberatung marriage counselling

Eheberatungsstelle marriage guidance centre

eheliche Gemeinschaft conjugal relationship, marital relationship

Ehelich(keits)erklärung (jur., obsolet) declaration of legitimacy (of an illegitimate child upon the father's application)

ehemündig (jur.) capable to marry, of marriageable age

Eheversprechen engagement, promise to marry

Ehevertrag marriage contract

Ehre honour

Ehrenamt honorary office

ehrenamtlich tätig sein (v.) to serve in an honorary capacity

ehrenamtlich tätig sein im sozialen Bereich (Freiwilligenarbeit) voluntary work, caring services

eidesstattliche Versicherung statutory declaration

Eigenanteil (s.S.) ⇒ Selbstbeteiligung

Eigenvorsorge, kollektive collective (or group) private provision

Eigenbedarf personal use

Eignungstest aptitude test

einbezogen involved

Einbürgerung naturalisation

Einelternfamilie single-parent family, lone parent family

Einfühlungsvermögen empathy

Einführung induction

Eingewöhnung (Arbeitsplatz, Umgebung) familiarisation, assimilation, induction

Eingewöhnung (Ausländer) adjutment, integration

Eingewöhnung (Heim, Wohnort) acclimatisation

Eingliederung (Behinderte, Ausländer, Umsiedler) integration, rehabilitation

Eingliederungshilfe (Behinderte) integration facilities, rehabilitation aid (for disabled person)

Einkommen, verfügbares disposable income

Einkommens- und Vermögenspüfung means test, (lit., earnings and assets test)

Einkommensersatzleistung income replacement benefit

Einkommensgrenze income limit

Einkommensprüfung (soz.) assessment of earnings

einkommensschwach low income, economically vulnerable

Einkommensverteilung income distribution

Einreichen (Beschwerde) file (a complaint) (Gesuch) submit (a petition) (v.)

Einrichtungen (i.w.S.) (soz.) services, premises, facilities

Einrichtungen (i.e.S: Heime und Anstalten) (soz.) institutions, (Summe aller Angebote) (soz.) provisions

Einsatz von Einkommen und Vermögen (vor Inanspruchnahme von Sozialleistungen) putting income/assets to use, invest

Einschränkung (Leistungen) restriction, limitation, reduction, dock

Einschüchterung intimidation

Einsprache (A, CH) ⇒ Einspruch

Einspruch (adm., jur.) objection, protest, Einspruch einlegen lodge an appeal

einstellen (Verkauf, Zahlungen) suspend

Einstellung (Arbeitskräfte) recruitment, employment

Einstellung (Geisteshaltung) attitude

Einstellung (Verfahren) (adm., jur) suspension, stay, dismissal

einstimmig unanimous

Einstimmigkeit unanimity

Einwanderer immigrant

Einwanderung immigration

Einwilligung consent, (nach Aufklärung) informed consent

Einzelfallarbeit case work, see 🕮 social intervention

Einzelfallberatung individual counselling

Einzelfallgerechtigkeit (soz.) individual justice

Einzelfallhilfe (Problemlösung und/oder Problembewältigung mit Klienten und deren Familien) (soz.) casework

Elementarbereich (päd.) preschool and elementary or primary education (infant and junior grades, 5-11 years old)

Elementarbereich/Primärbereich (familienergänzende Erziehung, 3- bis 7-jährige) pre-school, pre-primary education- erziehung (päd.) elementary education

elterliche Sorge parental care

Eltern, biologische natural parents

Eltern-Kind-Beziehung parent-child relationship

Eltern-Kind-Gruppen parent-and-child groups

Elternarbeit work with parents

Elternbeirat (päd.) parents advisory council

Elternbeteiligung (USA: auch Mitwirkung an der Erteilung des Schulunterrrichts) parent participation, involvement

Elterninitiativen parents' initiatives

Elternrecht parental authority

Elternteil, sorgeberechtigter parent with custody

Empfänger (soz.) recipient, beneficiary, client

Empfängnisregelung fertility control

Empfängnisverhütung (Techniken) contraception

empirische Sozialforschung empirical social research

Engagement, soziales community involvement

Enkulturation (soziol.) enculturation

Entbindung (Entlastung von Pflichten) release, dispensation -(med.) delivery, giving birth

Entfremdung (psych., soz.) alienation

Entgelt renumeration

Entgeltvereinbarung agreement on renumeration

Entgiftung (von einem Suchtmittel) detoxification

Entgrenzung (Verwischung) blurring, delimitation

Entlassung (Gefangene) release, discharge (from prison)

Entlassung, bedingte ~ conditional release

Entlassung, vorzeitige ~ parole

Entlassung auf Bewährung release on probation (von Arbeitnehmern) ⇒ Kündigung

Entmündigung (jur.) declaration of disability, declaration of incapacity, declaration of legal incompetence (USA)

Entschädigung (jur.) compensation, indemnity, restitution

Entschädigung der Opfer von Gewalttaten indemnification of victims of violence, crime

Entschädigung, soziale social compensation

Entschädigungsrente compensatory pension

entscheiden decide, sich für etwas entscheiden opt for sth.

Entscheidung (adm.) decision

Entscheidungsbefugnis authority to make decisions, competence, jurisdiction

Entschuldung disencumbrance, reduction of indebtedness

Entwicklungsplanung development planning

Entscheidungspsychologie developmental psychology

Entscheidungsstörung (med., psych.) development disorder, retardation

Entwöhnung (Alkohol, Drogen) disaccustoming, habit breaking

Entziehung (Alkohol, Drogen) detoxification, treatment of addicts, drug withdrawal

Epilepsie epilepsy

Erbanlage gene(s) genetic trait, genotype

Erbe (Nachlass) heir, inheritor (estate)

Erbkrankheit hereditary disease, genetic disease

Erbrecht (jur. Kategorie) law of inheritance (descent, succession)

Erbrecht (persönliches) right of inheritance

Erbschaft inheritance, heritage, legacy

Erfolg success

Erhebung (stat.) survey

Erhebung einer Steuer levy

Erholungsurlaub recreational holiday

Erlass (jur.) writ, decree

erlassen (Bestimmung, Gesetze) issue

erlassen (Strafe, Schuld) release sb. from sth. (v.), acquit, go unpunished- (Verpflichtung, Kosten) dispense, exempt sb. From sth.

Erlebnispädagogik (in Irland auch von der Polizei eingesetzt) diversion project, adventure sports

Erlös proceeds

Ermächtigung authorisation

Ermäßigung (Eintritt, Beitrag) reduction, reduced, cut rate

Ermessen, pflichtgemäßes due regard

Ermessensentscheidung discretionary decision

Ermittlungsverfahren (jur.) preliminary proceedings

Ernährer/in (der Familie) bread winner

Ersatzanspruch (zwischen sozialen Leistungsträgern oder gegen verpflichtete andere) claim of compensation

Ersatzdienst ⇒Zivildienst

Ersatzfamilie (jun.) ⇒Pflegefamilie

Ersatzfamilie (sen.) substitute family

Ersatzkrankenkasse (s.S.) substitute health insurance fund (of public law nature)

entmutigen daunt

Erstattung reimbursement, refund

Erstattungsanspruch ⇒ Ersatzanspruch

Erstgespräch first session, initial contact

Ertrag proceeds, returns

Erwachsenenbildung adult education

Erwerbsbevölkerung (stat.) economically active population

Erwerbsersatz (Wehrdienst) (CH) ⇒ Unterhaltssicherung

Erwerbslosigkeit unemployment benefit

Erwerbstätigkeit (gainful) employment

Erwerbsunfähigkeit incapacity to earn a living

Erwerbsunfähigkeitsrente earning incapacity pension

Erzieher/in educator (päd.) early childhood educator, child development officer (USA)

Erziehung education, pedagogic, child rearing, bringing up a child, (Kleinkinder) upbringing of infants, rearing up children

Erziehungsanspruch (des Kindes) right to an adequate education

Erziehungsanstalt (veraltet) ⇒ Erziehungsheim

Erziehungsbeihilfe educational grant (or allowance)

Erziehungsbeistand(schaft) (jun.) supervision order by the youth office or the court to help and advise the persons having parental authority

Erziehungsberatung (Pflichtleistung der Gemeinden) (D) child guidance (statutory local service, UK, USA)

Erziehungsberatungsstelle child guidance clinic

Erziehungsberechtigte/r person having a right to bring up and educate a child, having parental authority

Erziehungsgeld (soz.) (D) child-rearing benefit, (child allowance, child benefit) ⇒ Kindergeld

Erziehungsheim correctional institution, "Borstal", approved school, detention centre, treatment centre reformatory (USA)

Erziehungshilfe (Fürsorgeerziehung) (residential) care, training in a borstal

Erziehungshilfe (jun.) child rearing support

Erziehungshilfe, freiwillige ~ (FEH) education advisory service, voluntary supervision

Erziehungsmaßnahmen educational measures-plan educational planning

Erziehungsregister register of public measures in child care

Erziehungsschwierigkeiten child rearing difficulties

Erziehungsurlaub (D) maternity/paternity leave, parental leave, educational leave (for mother or father of a new born child up to twelve months)

Erziehungswissenschaft pedagogy

Erziehungswissenschaftler/in educationalist

Erziehungszeit educational leave, parental leave

Erziehungsziele educational aims

Erziehungswissenshaft theory of education, pedagogy

Essen auf Rädern meals on wheels, home delivered meals (USA)

Etikettierungsansatz (soziol.) labelling approach

Existenzminimum subsistence level, breadline

Europäischer Freiwilligendienst European Voluntary Service

extramurale Versorgung (außerhalb eines psychiatrischen Krankenhauses) (D) community care (in German "extramural" refers to psychiatric hospitals only)

– F –

Fachaufsicht technical, professional supervision

Fachhochschule (für Sozialarbeiter, Sozialpädagogen) (D) college at university level (for social workers, social pedagogues), school of social work

Fachkrankenhaus specialised hospital

Fachlichkeit professionalism

Fachoberschule technical secondary school

Fachplanung expert planning, specialised planning

Fachschule (für Erzieher) specialist training college (for educators at elementary level)

Fähigkeit (bes. Behinderte) aptitude

Fahrdienste (für Behinderte) transportation sevies (for disabled people)

Fahrlässigkeit negligence, carelessness

Falle pitfall

Fallbericht case study, report

Fallbeschreibung case description

Fallbesprechung case conference

Fallstudie case study

familial family (upbringing, setting)

familial (soziol.) familial

Familie, unvollständige one-parent family

Familie, biologische biological family, family of origin

Familienalltag everyday family-life

Familienangehörige/r family member, dependent

Familienangehörige/r, mithelfende/r collaborating family member

Familienbeihilfe, Familienzuschlag family allowance

Familienberatung family counselling, family therapy

Familienberatungsstelle family advice centre (UK)

Familienbericht (D) Family Report

familienergänzende Hilfen supplementing family provisions

Familienermäßigung (Bahnfahrten, Eintritt usw.) family reduction, family rate (USA)

Familienfürsorge family welfare

familiengerechte Hilfe family-orientated assistance

Familiengericht family court

Familiengerichtshilfe family court assistance

Familienhilfe (s.S.) family support, welfare

Familienhilfe, sozialpädagogische sociopedagogic family aide

Familien(kranken)hilfe family allowance (or benefits)

Familienkrise family crisis

Familienlastenausgleich compensation for family duties

Familienorganisation family organisation, association

Familienpflege (sen., jun.) foster care

Familienpfleger/in (D) homehelp, housemaker, home health aide (USA)

Familienpflegestelle place in a foster family

Familienplanung family planning

Familienpolitik family policy

Familienrecht family law

Familienstand marital status

Familientherapie family therapy

Familienunterbringung (jun., sen.) family placement, (jun. auch) boarding out with a family (UK),

Familienunterhalt family maintenance

familienunterstützende und -ergänzende Hilfen family support, complementary measures

Familienzusammenführung reuniting (with) a family

Familienzuschlag family allowance

Fehlentscheidung false, erroneous decision

Feldforschung (soziol.) field research

feldorientierte Sozialarbeit patch social work

Festnehmen (v.) (Schaden, Hilfe, Gebühr) determine (a certain amount), assess, set, fix

festsetzen stipulate

Feststellung (Aussage) statement, declaration

Feststellung (Ermittlung) ascertainment, establishment of facts

Finalprinzip finality principle

Finanzausgleich financial equalization (between financially weak and strong entities: e.g. Länder of Communities)

Finanzierungsträger provider, source of finance (or funds)

Findelkind abandoned child, foundling

Fixer junkie

Flächennutzungsplan area development plan

flexible Altersgrenze flexible age limit, flexible pension age

Flüchtling refugee

föderalistisches System federal system

Folgekosten ensuing costs

Förderlehrgänge promotional courses

Forderung (jur.) claim

förderungsfähig eligible for promotion, sponsorship

förderungswürdig deserving of being promoted, sponsored

Fortbildung, laufende further education, (im bisherigen Berufsfeld, Weiterbildung) continuing education, training

Frauenarbeitsschutz protection of working women

Frauenberufe typical female occupations

Frauenbewegung women's (liberation) movement

Frauenfragen women's concerns

Frauenförderprogramm programme to promote women

Frauengleichstellung equality of women

Frauengleichstellungsverordnung regulation on gender equality

Frauenhaus house for battered women, women's refuge, Women's Aid Centre

Frauenrechtler/in feminist

Freibetrag, steuerlicher tax allowance

Freie Träger voluntary (welfare) agencies

Freie Wohlfahrtsflege non-statutory welfare

Freigänger prisoner on day release (for work/study)

Freigrenze capital, earnings disregard

Freiheitsbeschränkung restriction of freedom

Freiheitsentziehung (psychisch Kranke) committal, involuntary admission

Freiheitsentzug, lebenslänglicher (jur.) imprisonment

Freistellung exemption, (militärisch) release

freiwillige Versicherung voluntary insurance

freiwilliges soziales Jahr (D) Voluntary Year of Social Service (one year of voluntary community service)

Freizeit time-off, spare time, leisure

Freizeitbetreuung supervised leisure activities, play scheme

Freizeitgesellschaft leisure society

Freizeitgestaltung leisure time activities

Freizeitpädagogik leisure time education,pedagogics

Freizügigkeit(srecht) (right to) free movement

Fremdplatzierung (jun.) placement outside the natural family

Fremdwahrnehmung (psych.) hetero-perception, ectoperception

Friedenserziehung peace education

Frist time limit, stipulated period

Fristablauf expiry of time limit

Fristverlängerung extension of time limit

Früherkennung (med.) early detection, diagnosis

Frühförderung Behinderter early health promotion and support for handicapped people

Frühinvalidität (s.S.) disablement before retirement age

frühkindliche Entwicklung early childhood development

frühkindliche Hirnschädigung cerebral palsy (perintal brain damage)

Frühpension (A) ⇒ Altersruhegeld, vorzeitiges

Frührentner early retirement pensioner

Führungsaufsicht supervision of conduct

Führungszeugnis reference, polizeiliches Führungszeugnis clearance

Fürsorge care, assistance, welfare

Fürsorgeerziehung (FE) residential care, residential training in a borstal

Fürsorgepflicht duty of care

Fürsorgeprinzip welfare principle

Fürsorgewesen social welfare, public (social) assistance (USA)

– G –

Garantien sozialer Rechte guarantee of social rights

Gebärdensprache (Minderheitensprache, nicht zu verwechseln mit einer "technischen Hilfssprache") sign language 🕮 sign language

Gebietskörperschaft territorial authority

Gebrechen infirmity, physical or mental disability

gebrechlich frail, infirm

Gebrechlichkeitspflegschaft (jur.) curatorship ordered in case of physical or mental disability

Gebührenpflichtig (adm.) subject to fees, liable for a fee, (gebührenpflichtige Strasse: toll road, gebührenpflichtige Verwarnung: fine)

Geburtendefizit birth deficit, inadequate birth rate

Geburtenrückgang falling birthrate

Gefährdete/r (soz.) person at risk

Gefährdetenhilfe services to people at risk

Gefühl feeling, emotion (Erregung), sentiment (Empfindung), touch (Tastsinn)

Gefühlsarbeit emotional labour

Geheimhaltungspflicht obligation to maintain secrecy

Geheimnisschutz (⇒ Schweigepflicht) (jur.) privilege of privacy

Gehirnschaden (med.) cerebral damage, brain damage

Gehorsamspflicht duty to be loyal

Geisteskrankheit (med.) mental illness

geistig behindert mentally disabled

geistig Behinderte mentally disabled people

geistige Behinderung mental disablement, handicap

geistige Gesundheit mental health

gelähmt paralysed

Gelassenheit serenity

Geld money

Geldleistung (soz.) cash benefit

Geldstrafe fine

Geldverlegenheit financial embarassment

Gelegenheitsarbeit casual labour, work, odd job

Gemeinde (religiöse) congregation

Gemeinde (Verwaltungsbezirk) municipality

Gemeinde (Verwaltungsstelle) local authority

Gemeindekrankenpflege (außerhalb von Heimen, Anstalten) community health care

gemeindenahe Betreuung (d.h. nicht in Heim oder Anstalt) community care (as opposed to institutional care), out patient services

Gemeindepsychiatrie community psychiatry

Gemeindeschwester community nurse, public health nurse

Gemeindeverwaltung municipality

Gemeindezentrum community centre

Gemeindeentwicklung community development

Gemeindeplanung community planning

gemeinnützige Arbeit work in the public interest

gemeinnützige Organisation non-profit organisation

Gemeinnützigkeit charitable status

Gemeinschaftseinrichtung community provision, facility

Gemeinsinn sense of community

Gemeinwesenarbeit (soz.) community work 📖 social intervention

Gemeinwirtschaft non-profit sector (business sector under special social obligations, profit restricted, publicly assisted or tax privileged)

Gemeinwohl common weal, public weal

gemütskrank affect disorder

genehmigen (v.) authorize, approve

Genehmigung permission, licence, permit

genehmigungspflichtig (adm.) subject to approval

Generationenkonflikt generation conflict

Generationenvertrag (D) intergenerational treaty

Genetik genetics

genetische Beratung genetic counselling

genetisches Gutachten (Vaterschaft) genetic (paternity) test

Genossenschaft cooperative

Geriatrie geriatrics

gerichtliche Entscheidung court decision, judicial ruling

Gerichtsbarkeit jurisdiction

Gerichtsbarkeit, freiwillige jurisdiction over non-contentious matters

Gerichtsbeschluss court order

Gerichtsverhandlung hearing, trial, proceedings

Gerontopsychiatrie geriatric psychiatry, gerontopsychiatry

Gesamtplan (Rehabilitation) master plan

Gesamtvereinbarungen (Behindertenhilfe) comprehensive agreements

Geschäfts(un)fähigkeit (jur.) legal (in) competence (USA)

Geschäftsführung management

Geschäftsführer/in manager

Geschäftsräume premises

Geschäftsstelle office, branch

Geschlecht sex (biologisch), gender (soziales Konstrukt)

Geschlechtskrankheit sexually transmitted disease (WHO), venereal, sexual disease

geschlechtsspezifisch sex specific, gender specific

Gesetz law, act, law, regulation 🕮 law

Gesetz (einzelnes) (z.B. Bundessozialhilfegesetz) (D) act, statute (e.g. Federal Public Welfare Act)

Gesetz und Recht (oder Rechtsgebiet) (z.B. Sozialhilferecht) (D) law (e.g. public welfare law)

Gesetzbuch code

Gesetz, Einhaltung des compliance with the law, conformity with the law

Gesetzesänderung amendment

Gesetzesübertretung offence

Gesetzesvorlage bill

Gesetzgebungszuständigkeit legislative competence

gesetzliche/r Vertreter/in statutory representative

Gesprächsführung, Methoden der ~ interviewing methods, skills

Gesuch application, petition

Gesundenuntersuchung (A) ⇒ Vorsorgeuntersuchung

Gesundheit health

Gesundheitsamt (local) health authority, (Irl) Health Board (UK)

Gesundheitsdienst, öffentlicher public health services

Gesundheitshilfe health services

Gesundheitsvorsorge preventive health care

Gesundheitswesen, öffentliches public health services

Gewaltenteilung separation of powers

Gewalttätigkeit (act of) violence

Gewalttätigkeit gegen Ehegatten (⇒ Misshandlung) marital violence

gewichten weigh

Gewissensfreiheit freedom of conscience

Girokonto current account

Glaube faith, (Überzeugung) belief (an, in), (in gutem Glauben) in good faith

Gläubiger/in creditor (selten: believer, the faithful)

Gleichaltrige/r, **Gleichgestellte/r** peer group

Gleichbehandlung equal treatment

Gleichbehandlungsgrundsatz principle of equal treatment, as well: ban on discrimination

Gleichberechtigung equal rights, equality of status, equal entitlement

Gleichheits(grund)satz (jur.) equality before the law

Gleichstellung equal opportunities

Gnadengesuch petition, pardon for clemency

Graduierung (akademisch) graduation, conferring of a degree

Graduierung (Skala) gradation

Grenzfall boundary, borderline case

Großfamilie extended family

Grundbedürfnisse basic needs

Grundeinkommen ⇒ Volksrente

Grundpflege (⇒ Behandlungspflege) (med.) basic nursing

Grundrechte basic human rights

Grundrechte, soziale basic social rights

Grundrente (vor allem an Kriegsbeschädigte) (D) non means-tested basic pension (e.g. for war victims)

Grundversorgung (med.) primary health care (WHO)

Gruppenarbeit group work

Gruppendynamik group dynamics, interaction

Gruppenpädagogik group pedagogics

Gruppenprozess group process

Gruppentherapie group therapy, treatment

Gutachten expert opinion, report, expertise

Gutachter/in consultant, (sworn) expert

Gutschein voucher

– H –

Haftbefehl warrant

Haftung (jur.) liability, guarantee

Handlungsvollmacht authority to act

Hafturlaub ⇒ Sozialurlaub

Haltung (Einstellung) attitude

Haltung (inneres Gleichgewicht) composure

Haltung bewahren (v.) maintain one's composure

Handlungsfähigkeit (jur.) ⇒ Deliktsfähigkeit ⇒ Geschäftsfähigkeit

Handlungskompetenz operational competence, authority

Handlungsvollmacht authority to act

Härtefall (case of) hardship

Härtefallregelung hardship clause

Hauptfürsorgestelle (D) main welfare office for war victims and severely handicapped

Hausaufgabenhilfe help with homework, tutoring (USA)

Hausbesuch call, home visit

Hausbrandbeihilfe (soz.) winter fuel subsidy, heating allowance

Hausgrundstück, kleines (geschütztes Vermögen) (soz.) (D) small house and plot (disregarded in means test) (UK)

Haushaltsangehörige members of a household

Hausgemeinschaft household, house community

Haus(halts)hilfe (soz.) housekeeping assistance

Haushaltsvorstand head of household

Hauspflege (soz.) homehelp, nursing, homemaker service

Hauspflegerin ⇒ Familienpflegerin

Hausrat household equipment, effects

häuslich domestic

häusliche Erziehung upbringing at home, in the family

häusliche (Kranken)Pflege home care, nursing

Hebamme midwife

Heilbehandlung ⇒ Behandlung, ärztliche

heilen (v.) cure, heal

Heilerzieher/in (D) therapeutic educator

Heilerziehung (psych., päd) therapeutic education

Heilerziehungspfleger/in (D) special training personell (for handicapped and infirm persons)

Heilgymnastik remedial gymnastics

Heilhilfsberufe professions auxiliary to medicine

Heilmittel remedy (WHO)

Heilpädagog/e/in therapeutic educator, educational therapist

Heilpädagogik therapeutic pedagogy, eduction

heilpädagogische Einrichtung orthodpedagogical institution

Heilpflegestelle orthodpedagogic foster place

Heilsarmee Salvation Army

Heim home, institution, hostel

Heim (Wohnheim einer Anstalt, z.B. für Krankenschwestern, Studenten) residence

Heimarbeit home work

Heimaufsicht control and supervision of residential institutions

Heimbeirat advisory council in a home

Heimdifferenzierung (a provision of a) systematic variety of homes

Heimeinweisung institutionalisation

Heimerzieher/in residential (child) care worker

Heimerziehung (jun.) residential care

Heimleiter house parent, warden

Heimleiterin matron

Heimsonderschulen special residential schools

Heimunterbringung residential care

Heimvertrag home admission contract

Heimatprinzip (Soziahilfe, veraltet) principle of birth place in social welfare (obsolete)

Heiterkeit serenity

Heizungsbeihilfe (winter fuel) heating expenses subsidy, fuel allowance

helfende Beziehung caring relationship

helfende Berufe helping, caring professions

Helfer (Laien) (soz.) nonprofessional carers, helpers

Helferdienste, ehrenamtliche voluntary welfare services

Helferkonferenz care conference

Helfersyndrom helper syndrom

Hemmung inhibition

Heranwachsende/r adolescent, young adult

Herausgabe der Kinder handing over of children

Herausnahme (aus der Familie) removal (of a child from his/her family)

Herausnahme (aus Heimen, Anstalten, Anstaltswesen) deinstitutionalization (into community care)

Herausnahme (aus Jugendstrafvollzug) diversion

Herkunftsfamilie family of origin

Herumtreiber (Streuner) loiterer

Hilfe (soz.) aid, assistance, support

Hilfe in besonderen Lebenslagen assistance in critical life situations (e.g. sickness, inability, social assistance)

Hilfe zum Lebensunterhalt (Sozialhilfe) subistence benefit (social assistance)

Hilfe zur Selbsthilfe (soz.) aid towards independent living

Hilfe, persönliche personal social help, support, human services (USA)

Hilfsbedüftigkeit in need of assistance

Hilfeempfänger (soz.) welfare recipient, client

Hilfesuchender applicant, a person seeking help

Hilfsmittel (Geräte) (med.) appliances, aids

Hilfsquellen (adm.) resources

Hilfssystem (soz.) social support system

Hilfssystem, informelles informal social support system, network

Hilfswerk charitable organization

Hinterbliebene (s.S.) surviving dependent(s), bereaved (family)

Hinterbliebenenrente (s.S) survivors' pension, dependent's pension

Hinterlassene (CH) ⇒ Hinterbliebene

Hirnschädigung brain damage

Hirnschädigung, frühkindliche cerebral palsy

HIV human immune deficiency virus

homosexuell (Frauen) lesbian

homosexuell (i.w.S.) homosexual

homosexuell (Männer) gay

Honorar fee, (Autorenhonorar) royalty

Hörbehinderung hearing defect, hearing impairment

Hort (für Kinder) day-centre for school children, after school club

Hospitation hospitation, observation (visit)

Hospiz hospice

Humanisierung (Arbeitswelt, Strafvollzug etc.) humanisation (working life, prisions)

humanitäre Hilfe humanitarian relief aid

humanitäre Hilfen humanitarian relief actions

Hungerhilfe famine relief

Hygiene, psychische ⇒ Psychohygiene

– I –

Ideenwettbewerb competition of ideas, contest of ideas

Imitation mimicry

Impfschaden adverse effect of vaccination

Inanspruchnahme demand, claim, utilization

Indikation (med., psych.) indication

Indikation, medizinische, genetische, soziale (Schwangerschaftsunterbrechung) (abortion on) medical, genetic, social grounds

Individualisierungsprinzip (soz.) principle of individualised assistance

Informationspflicht duty to furnish information, obligation to notify

informeller Sektor ⇒ Schattenwirtschaft 🕮 informal economy

Infrastruktur, soziale network of services, provisions

Initiative initiative

In-Kraft-Treten coming into force

Innendienst (Sozialarbeiter) office, intake duty

Innenstadtsanierung inner city regeneration

Innenstadtverödung inner city decay

Innungskrankenkasse (guild) occupational insurance scheme

Insasse (veraltet) inmate, teils: resident

Institutionsberatung advice to institutions, consultancy

Integration integration

integrative Erziehung education aimed at and practicing social integration

Interaktion interaction

Interesse interest

Interesse, persönliches vested interest

Interessengruppe pressure group, interest group, vested interests (Interessengruppen)

interkulturell crosscultural, transcultural, intercultural

interkulturelles Lernen cross-cultural learning

internalisieren (v.) internalise

Internat boarding school

international (grenzüberschreitend) transnational

international (weltweit: Organisationen, Aktivitäten) global, universal

international (i.w.S. und völkerrechtlich) international

international (Regierungsgremium) inter-governmental

Interventionsstrategie intervention strategy

Intimsphäre privacy, private life

intramurale Versorgung (psych.) institutional psychiatric care

Invalidität invalidity, disability

Investition, soziale investment in social welfare

Inzest incest

– J –

Jahrgänge (stat.) cohort(s)

Jahrgänger (A, CH) ⇒ Gleichaltrige

Jugend youth, young people, the young, selten noch: juveniles, mit besonderem Bezug z.B. zu **jugendlicher Straftäter** young offender

Jugendalter youth, adolescence

Jugendamt (D) child (and youth) welfare office

Jugendarbeit (jun., päd.) youth work

Jugendarbeitslosigkeit youth unemployment

Jugendarbeitsschutz youth employment protection

Jugendarrest ⇒ Jugendstrafe

Jugendaustausch, internationaler World Youth Exchange (in Young Men's Christian Association)

Jugendbande gang of youngsters

Jugendberatung (D) counselling services for young people

Jugendbericht (D) Youth Report

Jugendbildung (D) out-of-school, extracurricular education

Jugendeinrichtungen provisions for young people, juvenile facilities (USA)

Jugenderholung recuperative holidays for young people, holiday schemes for the young

Jugendfreizeitstätten recreational centres, leisure time centres for young people

Jugendfürsorge (vorbeugende, schützende, heilende Massnahmen für einzelne junge Menschen in Gegenüberstellung zur Jugendpflege) youth welfare (preventive, protective and therapeutic measures for individual children and young people, as opposed to leisure time provision for the young)

jugendgefährdend(e Schriften, Filme) (literature, cinema-shows) likely to be harmful to young people

Jugendgericht juvenile court, young offenders' court

Jugendgerichtsbarkeit juvenile justice

Jugendhelfer/in guardian ad litem (UK), law guardian (USA)

Jugendhilfe social enquiry in juvenile cases

Jugendhaus youth centre, club

Jugendherberge youth hostel (travel accommodation)

Jugendhilfe (D) totality of German youth welfare services, youth services (UK), youth programs, child welfare (up to 18) (USA)

Jugendhilfegesetze youth welfare laws

Jugendhilfeplanung (D) youth welfare planning

Jugendhilfeträger youth welfare agencies

Jugendkriminalität juvenile delinquency

Jugendleiter/in ⇒ Sozialpädagoge

jugendlich (jur., med.) juvenile

jugendlich (soz.) young, youthful

jugendliche/r Straftäter/in juvenile delinquent

Jugendpflege (D) (in Gegenüberstellung zur Jugendfürsorge) youth welfare (leisure time pro-vision, as opposed to welfare work for the young), Youth and Community Service (in the educational system) (UK)

Jugendpfleger/in youth welfare worker

Jugendpläne youth development plans

Jugendprotest youth protest

Jugendreligion, Jugendsekte youth cult

Jugendring (D) (federal) association of youth organisations

Jugendschutz (legal) youth protection (in public)

Jugendsozialarbeit social work with children and young people

Jugendstaatsanwalt juvenile court prosecutor, legal presenting officer (USA)

Jugendstrafanstalt borstal, remand home, detention centre, juvenile prison (UK), reformatory, reform school (USA)

Jugendstrafe detention, corrective measures, reformatory, correctional measures (USA)

Jugendstrafrecht criminal law relating to juveniles

Jugendstrafvollzug custodial treatment of young offenders

Jugendverbände youth organizations

Jugendvertreter/in (im Betriebsrat) youth representative (on works council)

Jugendwohlfahrtsbehörden youth welfare authorities

Jugendwohngemeinschaften communal living of young people

Jugendwohnheim hostel for young people

Jugendzelle (statt Jugendstrafanstalt, Zelle im Bezirksgefängnis) (CH) prison cell for juvenile offenders

Jugendzentrum youth centre

Jugendzentrumsbewegung movement for the provision of youth centres

– K –

Kammer (Gericht, große Kammer) court in full

Kammer (Gericht, kleine Kammer) partial session

Kann-Leistung discretionary service, benefit

Karenzurlaub (A) ⇒ Mutterschaftsurlaub

Kassenarzt doctor participating in a health insurance plan

Kassenpatient/in social insurance patient, National Health (NH) patient (UK), Medicare patient (USA), panel patient (obsolete)

Katamnese catamnesis

Kaufkraft purchasing power

Kausal(itäts)prinzip principle of causality (or causation)

Kernfamilie ⇒ Kleinfamilie

Kind child

Kinderarbeitsverbot ban on child labour

Kinderarzt/~ärztin paediatrician, paediatrist

Kinderbetreuung care for children

Kinderdorf children's village

Kindererziehung child-rearing, education of children, child development

kinderfeindlich (Person) hostile to children

kinderfeindlich (Umgebung) unfit for children

kinderfreundlich (Person) fond of children

kinderfreundlich (Umgebung) suitable for children

Kindergarten (jun.) day nursery, children's day care centre, kindergarten

Kindergarten (päd.) preschool playgroup, nursery school, occasionally: Montessori school

Kindergartenhelfer/in (jun.) nursery aid

Kindergartenleiter/in (jun., päd.) head of nursery school

Kindergärtnerin (veraltet) ⇒ Erzieher

Kinderfürsorge child welfare

Kindergeld child benefits, children's allowance (non contributory) ⇒ Erziehungsgeld

Kindergeldkasse beim Arbeitsamt (D) child benefit fund at the labour office

Kinderhaus (innerhalb einer Institution) children's cottage, residence

Kinderheim children's home (institution)

Kinderkrankenschwester (med.) paediatric nurse

Kinderkrippe (päd.) day nursery (0-3 years), crèche

Kinderladen (D) "children's shop", anti-authoritarian Kindergarten

kinderlos childless, without children

Kinderpflegerin nurse

Kinderprostitution child prostitution

Kinderschutz child protection

Kinderschwester children's nurse

Kindertagesstätte, heilpädagogische day treatment centre for children

Kinder- und Jugendberatungsstelle child guidance clinic

Kinder- und Jugenderholung (jun.) recuperative holidays for children and young people

Kinder- und Jugendpsychiatrie child psychiatry

Kinderzulage child allowance

Kinderzuschuss child allowance or supplement

Kindesmisshandlung child abuse

Kindesvernachlässigung child neglect

Kindeswohl welfare of the child, best interests of the child

Klage (zivilrechtlich) (jur.) action, suit (USA)

klagen (jur.) bring an action against someone, sue someone, (sich allgemein beklagen complaining', lament

Kläger (jur.) plaintiff

Kleinfamilie nuclear family

Kleinkind infant, small child, (Krabbelalter) toddler

klientenzentriert client-centered

klinische Psychologie clinical psychology

knapp scarce

knappschaftliche Rentenversicherung miners' pensioninsurance (scheme)

knappschaftliche Krankenversicherung miners' health insurance (scheme)

Koedukation co-education

kollektive Eigenvorsorge collective self-provision

Kollektivvereinbarung collective agreement

kommerzielle Dienste, Einrichtungen (med., soz., jur.) private welfare sector, welfare industry

Kommunalaufsicht supervision of the local authorities/ municipalities by the state

Kommunale Selbstverwaltung decentralisation, administrative autonomy at local level

kommunale Spitzenverbände central associations of local authorities

Kommunalverwaltung local administration, municiality

Kompetenzkonfikt (jur.) conflict of authority

komplementäre Dienste und Einrichtungen für psychisch Kranke integrated services and provisions for psychiatric patients

Konfliktberatung (bes. Vor Schwangerschaftsabbruch) (soz.) conflict counselling

Konkubinat (CH) ⇒ eheähnliche Gemeinschaft

Konsumentenkredit consumer credit

Konsumentenverhalten consumer behaviour

kontaktarm withdrawn, unsociable

Kontaktaufnahme (soz.) outreach

kontaktfreudig out-going

Kontrakt contract

körperbehindert physically disabled

Körperersatzstück artificial limb, organ

Körperschaft corporation

Körperschaft des öffentlichen Rechts public corporation, body corporate under public law

Körpersprache body language

Kosten costs

Kostenbefreiung exemption from costs

Kostenbeitrag cost contribution

Kostenbeteiligung (s.S.) cost contribution according to relevant circumstances

Kostendämpfung (s.S.) cost containment

Kostenersatz reimbursement

Kostenerstattung (zwischen Sozial-leistungsträgern) restitution, refunding of expenditure

Kosten-Nutzen-Analyse cost-benefit analysis

Kostensatzvereinbarung agreement on assessment (and sharing) of costs

Kostenträger agency bearing financial responsibility

Kostgeld (CH) ⇒ Pflegesatz

Krabbelstube day-centre for toddlers, crèche

Krankenberufe nursing professions (medical)

Krankengeld (s.S.) sickness benefit (UK), temporary disablement compensation (USA)

Krankengeschichte anamnesis, case history

Krankengymnastik ⇒ Heilgymnastik

Krankenhaus hospital

Krankenhaus, psychiatrisches psychiatric, mental hospital

Krankenhausbedarfsplanung hospital supply planning

Krankenhauspflegesatz basic hospital charges

Krankenhilfe (soz.) sick benefit (public assistance)

Krankenkasse, gesetzliche statutory health insurance fund, public health funds

Krankenkasse, private private health insurance

Krankendienste nursing services

Krankenpflege nursing of the sick

Krankenpfleger/in (registered) nurse

Krankenschein health insurance certificate, medical card (für Personen mit geringem Einkommen, bei denen die Kosten öffentlich getragen werden)

Krankenschwester trained (registered) nurse

Krankenstation hospital ward, unit

Krankenversicherung (s.S.) health insurance (fund)

Krankenversicherung, gesetzliche statutory (social) health insurance

Krankenversicherung, private private health insurance (company)

krankhaft pathological, morbid

Krankheit sickness, illness, ailment, complaint, disease

Krebsvorsorge cancer prevention and early diagnosis

Kreis district (UK), county (USA)

Kriegsbeschädigter war invalid

Kriegsdienst ⇒ Wehrdienst

Kriegshinterbliebene surviving dependents of servicemen and war victims

Kriegsopfer war victims

Kriegsopferfürsorge welfare for war victims

Kriegsopferverbände associations of war victims

Kriegsopferversorgung public maintenance for war victims

Krippe (jun.) crèche

Krisenintervention crisis intervientIon

Kumulation von Ansprüchen (s.S.) multiple tier system of claims

Kündigung termination, idsmissal

Kündigung, fristlose summary dismissal

Kündigungsschutz protection against dismissal

Kündigung im Mietrecht protection of tenancy (against eviction)

Künstlersozialversicherung (d) social insurance for self-employed artists (health and pension)

Kur (Badekur) cure, course of treatment (at a health resort, spa)

Kuratorium (i.e.S.) board of trustees

Kuratorium (i.w.S.) committee

Kurzarbeit short-time work

Kurzarbeitergeld subsidy for short-time working

Kürzung (Mittel, Leistung) cutback, reduction

– L –

Länderfinanzausgleich means of financial equalisation between the federal states

ländlich rural, the countryside

Laienhilfe (soz.) voluntary welfare work

Land (Bundesland) Federal State, mostly kept as Land and Länder respectively

Landesärzte für Behinderte (D) state physicians responsible for disabled people

Landesjugendamt (D) youth office of the/on the level of the Land

Landesjugendplan (D) youth plan on the level/of the Land

Landeskrankenhaus, psychiatrisches state psychiatric hospital

Landfahrer travelling people, gypies, tramp 🕮 traveller

Landesgemeinde (CH) non-urban parish, township

Landesgericht regional court

Landkreis rural district

Landstreicher/in vagrant

Langzeitpflege long-term practice placement

Lastenausgleich off-setting, equalization of burdens

Lebensbedarf, notwendiger subsistence

Lebensberatung (D) life skills counselling

Lebensbewältigung coping

Lebenserwartung life expectancy

Lebensgrundlage, materielle basic necessities of life

Lebenshaltungskosten cost of living

Lebenslage life course, life situation, living conditions

Lebensauf curriculum vitae

Lebensmittelhilfe (Sachleistung) (soz.) food relief, welfare food, internvention beef, butter (UK), food stamps (USA)

lebensmüde weary of life, tired of life, suicidal

Lebensstandard standard of living

Lebensunterhalt livelihood

Lebensunterhalt in Heimen (Soziahilfe, bei Kindern auch in Pflegefamilie durch Jugendamt) residential welfare allowances

Lebensunterhalt verdienen earn a living

lebenswichtig essential, vital

Lebensversicherung life assurance, endowment insurance, assurance

Lebensversicherung (Todesfall-) life insurance, assurance

Legasthenie ⇒ Lese-Rechtschreib-Schwäche

Legitimation legitimation

legitim legitimate (legal, nicht gesetzwidrig) lawful

Lehrling ⇒ Auszubildender

leiden suffer

Leidensdruck (psych.) weight of suffering, psychological distress

Leiharbeiter/in worker who is seconded to another agency

Leihmutter surrogate mother, rent breeder (USA)

Leistung (objektiv gemessen) performance

Leistung (persönliche Tüchtigkeit) proficiency, achievement

Leistungen (Bar~) (soz.) benefits in kind

Leistungen (Sachleistungen) (soz.) benefits in kind

Leistungen, immaterielle ~ (D) intangible benefits

Leistungen, materielle ~ (D) material benefits

Leistungen, nachrangige ~ (D) subsidiary benefits

Leistungen, soziale ~ social provisions

Leistungen, vorrangige ~ (D) priority benefits

Leistungsempfänger/in recipient (of benefits), welfare recipient

Leistungsgesellschaft achievement society

Leistungsträger (D) ⇒ Sozialleistungsträger

Leistungsvermögen capability, capacity

Leistungsvertrag service contract

Leitung (Betrieb) management

Leitung (Dienststelle) administration

Leitung – (i.S.v. Aufsicht) control, supervision, guidance

Leitung (Sitzung) chair (meetings)

Leitung (Veranstaltung) organisation

Lenkungsausschuss steering commitee

lernbehindert educationally subnormal (ESN)

Lernbehinderung mild retardation

Lernmittelfreiheit free use of educational materials or learning aids

Lernstörung learning disability, disorder

Lernziel (päd.) learning objective

Lese-Rechtschreib-Schwäche dyslexia

Leumundszeugnis ⇒ Führungszeugnis

Liniensystem line management, organisation delegatory system

Lohnfortzahlung (bei Krankheit) continued payment of wages/continued wage payments, sick pay

Lohnkostenzuschuss wage cost subsidy

Lohnpfändung (jur.) distraint of wages

Lohnsteuer (Arbeitnehmer) income tax

Los (Schicksal, Bürde) lot

– M –

Macht power

mächtig powerful

Männlichkeit masculinity, manliness, maleness

Mahnung reminder

Mahnverfahren proceedings for order to pay debts

Management Leitung eines Betriebes, Verwaltung

Mandat brief, mandate

Mangel deficiency, lack, shortage

Manteltarifvertrag general agreement on conditions of employment

Maßnahmen zur Beschäftigung und sozialen Eingliederung (Behinderte, jugendliche Arbeitslose) (D) provisions for employment and social integration (of handicapped, young unemployed people)

Medienpädagogik media education, education about media, education with media

Medikament medicine, drug

Medikamentenmissbrauch drug abuse

Medikamentensucht drug dependency

medizinische Rehabilitation medical rehabilitation

Mehrbedarf (gesetzlich geregelt für Alleinerziehende, Alte, Schwangere, Erwerbstätige u.a. Gruppen) (soz.) (D) additional need

Mehrebenensystem multi level governance

Mehrfachbehinderung multiple handicap, disability

Mehrleistung (z.B. Krankenkasse) additional benefit

Meldeamt registration office

Meldepflicht (adm.) obligation to register

Meldepflicht (med.) compulsory notification

Menschenhandel trafficking in people

Menschenkenntnis knowledge of human nature

Menschenverstand, allgemeiner (gesunder) common sense

Menschenwürde dignity of humankind, human dignity

Miete rent

Mieterschutz tenant protection, protected tenancy

Mietrecht tenancy law

Mietschulden rent arrears

Mietverhältnis tenancy

Mietzinsbeihilfe (A) ⇒ Wohngeld

Mietpreisbindung rent control, rent regulation

mildtätig ⇒ wohltätig

Milieu (Umgebung) milieu, social environment, social setting

Milieu (Umwelt, Halbwelt) underworld, demi-monde

Militärversicherung (s.S.) (CH) insurance of servicemen

Mimik facial expression

Minderheit (soziale Gruppe) minority (group)

Minderheit, ethnische ethnic minority

minderjährig under age, minor

Minderjährigenschutz protection of minors

Mindestarbeitsbedingungen minimum working conditions

Mindestnormen sozialer Sicherheit minimum standards for social security

Mindestrente minimum pension

Missbrauch (Amt) (jur.) malfeasance

Missbrauch (Macht, Recht, Gesetz) abuse, misuse (power, right, law)

Missbrauch, sexueller sexual abuse

Missbrauch von Finanzmitteln misapplication of funds

Misshandlung abuse, maltreatment, illtreatment

Misshandlung, körperliche physical abuse

Mitarbeitervertretung ⇒ Personalrat

Mitbestimmung (Arbeiter) (worker['s]) co-determination

Mitbestimmung (Eltern) parent participation

Mitbestimmung (Schüler) student participation in decision making

Mitteilungspflicht (Vermögen, Einkommen) (soz.) obligation to disclose (assets and income)

mittellos destitute

Mitverantwortung joint responsibility

Mitwirkung particiaption

Mitwirkungspflicht (soz.) obligation to cooperate

mobile Dienste mobile support services, service bus

Mühe effort, trouble

Multiplikator multiplier

Mündel ward

mündig of age

Mündigkeit full age, majority

Muße ⇒ Freizeit

Mussleistung ⇒ Pflichtleistung

Mutter-Kind-Einrichtung mother (parent) and baby provision

Mutterschaftsgeld, Mutterschaftshilfe (s.S.) maternity benefits

Mutterschaftsurlaub maternity leave

Mutterschutz maternity protection, protection of expectant and of nursing mothers

Mütterberatung mother and child consultation, counselling

Mütterberatungsstelle mother and infant clinic

Müttererholung recuperative holidays for mothers

Mutterpass medical record for mothers

Mutter- und Kinderschutz (med., soz.) maternal and child (health) care, maternal and child (health) care protection

– N –

Nachbarschaft (physische, auch im übertragenen Sinne) vicinity

Nachbarschaft (soziol.) neighbourhood

Nachbarschaftshilfe (informelle Initiative) neighbourhood scheme

Nachbarschaftszentrum neighbourhood centre

Nachbehandlung after-care

Nachfrage demand, request

nachgehende Hilfe (soz.) ⇒ Nachsorge

Nachholbedarf backlog demand

Nachlass estate, heritage

Nachlasspfleger/in (jur.) curator of an estate

Nachlasspflegschaft curatorship (of an estate)

Nachrang der Sozialhilfe (D) subsidiarity of public assistance

Nachrangprinzip principle of subsidiarity

Nachsorge (persönliche im Einzelfall im Anschluss an Hauptmaßnahme, z.B. der Rehabilitation) (soz., med.) aftercare

Nachuntersuchung (med.) re-examination

Nachmieter/in next tenant

Nachtklinik night hospital

Nachtwache night duty

Nachtarbeit night work

Nachtschicht night shift

nahrhaft nourishing, nutritious

Naturalleistungen ⇒ Sachleistung

Nebenkosten additional expenses

Nebenwirkung side-effect

Neigungsgruppe common interest group

Nervenheilanstalt (veraltet) ⇒ Psychiatrische Klinik

Neurologie neurology

Neurose neurosis

nichtehelich (Kind) (jur.) illegitimate, out-of-wedlock

nichtig invalid (ungültig), trivial (belanglos), vain (wertlos)

Nichtigkeitserklärung annulment

Nichtsesshafte/r homeless person, sb. with no fixed abode, without place of residence, tramp

Nichtsesshafte (Gruppe) homeless (people)

Nichtsesshaftenhilfe assistance to people with no fixed bode

Nichtsesshaftigkeit homelessness

nichtstaatlich non-statutory, non-governmental

Niedriglohn low-wage

Nießbrauch usufruct

Not destitution in, “below the breadline”, in dire need

Notaufnahme emergency admission

Notdienst emergency service

Notfall emergency

Notrufanlage (bas. Sen.) emergency alarm, hot line

Notstands(aus)hilfe(A) ⇒ Arbeitslosenhilfe, Sozialhilfe

Notunterkunft emergency shelter

Notzucht ⇒ Vergewaltigung

nutzen utilise

Nutzung (sozialer Angebote) utilisation, take-up (of social provisions)

– O –

Obdach shelter

Obdachlos/e homeless (people), vagrants (eher US), tramp (eher US)

Obdachlosenhilfe assistance to homeless people

Obdachlosenunterkunft hostel, shelter for homeless people

Obdachlosigkeit homelessness

Obergrenze ceiling, upper limit

Oberschule secondary school

Obhut care, keeping ⇒ Personensorge

Objektivität (Sachlichkeit) objectivity

Objektivität (Tatsächlichkeit) factuality

Objektivität (Unparteilichkeit) impartiality

Obrigkeit authority

offenbaren (offenlegen) (v.) disclose, divulge

Offenbarung revelation

Offenbarungspflicht obligation to disclose

offene Hilfe (frei zugänglich, insbes. jun., sen.) (freely accessible), open-door provisions

offene Hilfe (nichtstationär) community care 🕮: social intervention

offene Jugendarbeit non-institutional youth work

offene Stelle vacancy

öffentliche Erziehung public education

öffentliche Träger public agencies

öffentliches Recht public law

Öffentlichkeitsarbeit public relations

örtlicher Träger local agency

Ohrfeige slap

Opfer von Gewalttaten victims of violence, crime

Opferentschädigung indemnification of victims

Ordner (z.B. bei Demonstrationen) steward

ordnen order, organise

Ordnungsverwaltung administration of public order

Ordnungswidrigkeit (jur.) administarttive offence

Orientierungshilfe guide-line assistance

orthopädische Hilfsmittel orthopaedic aids

orthopädische Versorgungsstellen agencies for orthopaedic services

örtliche Zuständigkeit local responsibility, competence

örtlicher Träger local agency

ortsansässig resident, local

Ortschaft locality, village

– P –

Pacht lease

Pädagoge/Pädagogin education(al)ist, teacher, educator (US)

Pädagogik pedagogy, pedagogics, science of education

Pakt pact, agreement

Parität parity, equality

paritätisch (häufig: konfessionsfrei) in equal numbers, on equal terms, non-denominational non-sectarian

parteiisch biased, partial

Patient/in patient

Patientenfürsprecher/in (Krankenhaus) (CH) 'patients' advocate (hospital)

Pauschale (festgesetzter Beitrag) flat rate

Pension ⇒ Altersruhegeld

Personalakte report, personal file

Personalrat works council, worker's council

Personensorge (jur.) parental responsibility for the child

Personenstand ⇒ Familienstand

Personenstandsregister register of civil status, register of births, deaths and marriages (UK), register of births, marriages and burials (USA)

persönliche Bedürfnisse (des täglichen Lebens) personal needs in daily life, day-to-days needs

persönliche Betreuung personal care

persönliche Hilfe ⇒ Hilfe, persönliche

persönliches Interesse vested interest

Persönlichkeitsentwicklung personal development, development of the personality

Personalbüro personell office

Personaleinsparung staff saving, dismissal

Personalknappheit staff shortage

Personalmangel staff shortage

Personalversammlung staff meeting

Personalvertretungsgesetz negotiation rights (unionised), negotiation licence

Personensorge care and custody (of an individual)

pfänden (Gegenstände des Eigentums) seize sth. as pledge, distrain upon sth.

pfänden (Guthaben bei Dritten) garnish (an account)

Pfändung seizure of, distraint upon

Pfändungsschutz protection against attachment proceedings

Pflege foster care, nursing

Pflege chronisch Kranker long term care

Pflegeabteilung nursing ward, unit

Pflegebedürftigkeit, sozialversicherungsrechtliche Absicherung gegen das Risiko der Pflegebedürftigkeit (s.S.) insurance for long term nursing care

Pflegeeltern foster parents

Pflegeerlaubnis (jun.) foster child permit

Pflegefall permanent nursing case

Pflegefamilie foster family

Pflegegeld (Behinderte) insurance benefits or public assistance, benefits for payment of nursing care

Pflegegeld (bei häuslicher Pflege) long term care allowance, attendance allowance

Pflegegeld (Pflegekinder) fostering allowance

Pflegeheim nursing home

Pflegekind foster child

Pflegekinderaufsicht supervision of foster children

Pflegekinderwesen matters concerning foster children

Pflegekräfte (bes.sen.) professional attendants

Pflegepersonen (D) nonprofessional attendants

Pfleger/in (jur.) curator

Pfleger/in (med.) male nurse,ward attendant

Pflegesatz (Heime) (soz., jun.) daily allowance

Pflegesatz (Krankenhaus) (s.S.) hospital accommodation and treatment charges.

Pflegetage (Kankenhaus) patient days

Pflegeverhältnis fostering relationship

Pflegeversicherung long-term care insurance

Pflegevertrag fostering contract

Pflegezulage (vor allem an pflegebedürftige Kriegsbeschädigte) nursing allowance

Pflegschaft (Personen) curatorship, custodianship

Pflichtarbeitsplätze für Schwerbehinderte (D) legal obligation to provide jobs for disabled (persons)

Pflichtbeitrag (s.S.) compulsory contribution

Pflichtmitgliedschaft compulsory, obligatory membership

Pflichtteil (jur.) statutory portion

Pflichtversicherung (s.S.) compulsory insurance, statutory insurance

Pflichtverteidiger assigned counsel

Planspiel planning exercise

Planstelle (adm.) permanent post, (established post)

Planung planning

Planung, kurzfristige short range planning, short term planning

Planung, mittelfristige medium range planning, dedium term planning

Planung, langfristige long range planning, long term planning

Planungsabteilung planning department

Planungsberatung planning advice (centre)

Planungsebene planning level

Planungsgrundlagen planning elements, basic planning data

Planungsmethoden und -techniken planning methods and techniques

Planungsziel planning goal, objective

Politik (Politikbereich) policy, (Prozess) politics, (Institution) polity

Pluralität popularity

polizeiliches Führungszeugnis clearance

Populismus populism

Praktikant/in student on placement, trainee

Praktiker/in practitioner

Praktikum placement

praktisch bildbar (geistig Behinderte) capable of acquiring manual skills (mentally retarded)

Prävention prevention

Praxisanleitung, Praxisberatung supervision, supervised learning

Prämie award, grant

prämieren award, grant

Proband/in probationer

probewohnen (sen.) trial stay

Probewohnzeit probationary period

Prognose prognosis, forecast, projection

Produktionsweise mode of production

Produktivkräfte productive forces

Projekt project

Projektberatung project consultancy

Projektfinanzierung project financing

Prostitution prostitution

Protokoll, zu Protokoll geben state for the minutes

Prozess (Ablauf, Vorgang) process

Prozess (jur.) trial

Prozessgegner opposing party (in litigation)

Prozesskostenhilfe ("Armenrecht") legal aid

Prüfung examination

Psychagogik psychagogy

Psychiater/in psychiatrist

Psychiatrie psychiatry

Psychiatrie Enquete (D) commission of Inquiry into Psychiatric Services (1970-75)

psychische Krankheit mental illness

Psychoanalyse psychoanalysis

Psychoanalytiker/in psychoanalyst

psychogen psychogenic

Psychohygiene psychohygiene

Psychologe/Psychologin psychologist

Psychologie psychology

Psychose psychosis

psychosomatisch psychosomatics

psychosoziale Arbeitsgemeinschaften (psych.) (D) psychosocial working groups (coordination of services to facilitate the community care of mentally ill persons).

psychosoziale Diagnose psycho-social diagnosis

Psychotherapeut/in psychoterapist

Psychotherapie psychotherapy

– Q –

Qual pain, agony

quälen torment, torture

qualifizieren qualify

Qualität quality

Quelle source

quengelig grumpy, whining

querfeldein cross country

Querschnitt cross-section

Querschnittlähmung paraplegia

Querulant grouser, grumbler

Quittung receipt

Quote rate, quota

– R –

Rabatt discount

Rache revenge

radikal radical, drastic

Radikalkur drastic remedy

Rahmenbedingungen setting, framework, outline conditions

Randgruppe marginalised group, fringe group

Randgruppenarbeit social work with marginalised groups

Rationalisierungsschutzabkommen rationalisation protection agreement

Raumordnung area planning, territorial planning

Räumung eviciton

Räumungsbefehl (jur.) eviction order

Räumungsklage action for eviction

Rauschgift drugs, narcotics

Rauschgifthändler dealer, pusher

Rauschmittel (Drogen, Suchtmittel) intoxicant, dope

Razzia raid

Rechnungshof (adm.) audit office

Recht (insgesamt, auch Teilgebiete, z.B. Sozialrecht) law (social law)

Rechte, soziale welfare rights

rechtliches Gehör hearing in accordance with the law, day in court (USA)

Rechtsänderung amendment of law

Rechtsanspruch legal claim

Rechtsaufsicht control of legality

Rechtsbehelf legal remedy, relief, plea

Rechtsbehelfsbelehrung information concerning a person's remedies (against an order, etc.)

Rechtsberatung legal counselling

Rechtsberatungsstelle Legal Advice Centre

Rechtsfähigkeit legal capacity

Rechtshilfe (unter Gerichten ⇒ Amtshilfe) mutual judicial assistance

Rechtshilfeersuchen request for judicial assistance

Rechtskraft = res judicata validity

rechtskräftig (being) res judicata

Rechtsmittel legal redress, appeal

Rechtsmittelbelehrung being mode aware of one's rights (to appeal)

Rechtspflege administration of justice

Rechtspflicht legal duty, legal obligation

Rechtsprechung jurisdiction

Rechtsschutz protection of individual rights

Rechtsversicherung insurance covering legal charges

Rechtsstaat state in which the rule of law prevails

rechtsunwirksam ineffective, invalid

Rechtsverordnung regulation, statutory instrument 🕮 law

Rechtsvorschrift rule of law

Rechtsweg course of the law

rechtswidrig illegal, illegitimate, unlawful

Rechtswirksamkeit validity

Rechtswissenschaft jurisprudence

Redeweise jargon

Reform reform

Reformbemühung attempted reform

Regelbedarf (D) need as defined by official standard rates

Regelsatz official standard rates (social assistance)

Regionalplanung town and country planning

reglementieren regulate, regiment

Rehabilitation rehabilitation

Rehabilitation, berufliche vocational rehabilitation

Rehabilitation, Gesamtplan der ~ (D) overall rehabilitation plan, harmonization of rehabilitation measures

Rehabilitation, medizinische medical rehabilitation

Rehabilitation, schulische educational rehabilitation

Rehabilitation, soziale social rehabilitation

Rehabilitationsberater/in rehabilitation advisor, consultant

Rehabilitationsleistungen rehabilitation benefits

Rehabilitationsmaßnahmen rehabilitation measures

Rehabilitationsträger rehabilitation agency

Reisekostenabrechnung claim for travelling expenses

reizbar irritable, sensitive

reizen irritate, stimulate, provocate

Rente pension

Rente auf Zeit pension for a fixed period, temporary pension

Rente nach Mindesteinkommen (D) minimum pension (based on assumed minimum income)

Rentenalter pensionable, retirement age

Rentenanpassung adjustment of pensions

Rentenberechnung pension calculation

Rentenbemessungsgrundlage basis for the assessment of pensions

Rentenformel pensions formula

Rentenversicherung, freiwillige retirement pension, voluntary contribution to social insurance

Rentenversicherungsträger agencies of statutory pension insurance.

Rentnerkrankenversicherung health insurance for pensioners,

Repräsentativerhebung representative survey

Resozialisierung (im Strafvollzug) resocialisation (of delingquents)

Richtlinie directive, guiding instruction

Richtsatz scale of basic allowances

Richtwert (Planung) standard value

Risikogeburt high risk birth

Risikokinder (med.) delicate babies

risikobelastete Arbeit damage-prone work

Risikostrukturausgleich Risk Equalisation 🕮 Risikostrukturausgleich

Rollenerwartung (psych.) role expectation

Rollenkonflikt role conflict

Rollenspiel role play

Rollstuhl(benutzer) wheelchair (user)

Roma gipsies, Romanies

Rückerstattung restitution, reimbursement

Rückfall (Gewohnheit) relapse

Rückfall (med.) recurrence, relapse

Rückfall (Straftat) repeat offence

Rückfrage check back

Rücklage reserve, saving

rückwirkend retroactive, retrospective, dated back

Rückzahlung repayment, refund

Ruhestand retirement

– S –

Sachleistung benefit in kind

Sachverhalt circumstances, state of the case

Säuglingsausstattung layette, baby goods

Säuglingsfürsorge baby welfare, mother and child welfare

Säuglingsheim baby home

Säuglingspflege baby care

Säuglingssterblichkeit infant mortality (rate)

Säuglingstagesheim crèche, day nursery

Satzung constitution, statutes

Schadensersatz (jur.) damage compensation, restitution

Schattenwirtschaft shadow economy, black economy

Scheidung divorce

Scheidungsberatung divorce counselling

Schichtarbeit shift work

Schicht (Unter-, Mittel-, Oberschicht) (soziol.) social class (lower, middle, upper class), stratum

Schichtung, soziale social stratification

schichtspezifisch(e Erziehung) class specific (upbringing)

Schicksal (Bürde) lot

schikanieren harass

Schiedsstelle arbitrary board

Schlechtwettergeld bad weather allowance, intermittent unemployment insurance

Schlichtungskommission conciliation commission

schmähen revile

Schmerzensgeld (jur.) compensation for non-pecuniary (or immaterial) damage

Schnüffeldroge inhalant

schnüffeln (einer Droge) sniffing, inhaling

Schonvermögen (s.S.) certain assets (e.g. small home of one's own) for which no credit is available for social assistance

Schularbeitenhilfe Hausaufgabenhilfe

Schulden (haben) (to be in) debt

Schuldenerlass remission of debts

Schuldenregulierung regulation of debts

Schuldfähigkeit (strafrechtliche Verantwortlichkeit) criminal responsibility, accountability

Schuldfähigkeit (jur.) capability of guilty intent (mens rea, may be proved in children under the age of discretion)

Schuldnerberatung debt counselling

Schulpflicht, allgemeine compulsory education

Schulschwänzer truant

Schulsozialarbeit social work in schools, education welfare work

Schutzaufsicht (durch Änderung des KJHG durch 'Erziehungsbeistandschaft" ersetzt) protective supervision (replaced by "Erziehungsbeistandschaft" through an amendment of the Youth Welfare Act)

Schwangerschaft pregnancy

Schwangerschaftsabbruch Abortion, termination of pregnancy

Schwangerschaftskonfliktberatung pregnancy counselling

Schwarzarbeit labour/work in the black/shadow/informal economy

Schweigepflicht secrecy, professional discretion, confidentiality

Schwellenangst fear of entering

Schwerbehinderte, Arbeitsplatz für workplace for severely disabled persons

Schwerbehinderten, Eingliederung der ~ integration of disabled persons

Schwerbehindertenschutz protection of people with disabilities

Schwerbehinderte/r (Schwerbeschädigter) disabled person, handicapped person

schwererziehbar (veraltet) – verhaltensgestört, schwierig

Schwerstbehinderte/r person with an aggravated disablement or handicap

Schwerstpflegebedürftigkeit in need for most intensive care

schwul gay

seelish behindert emotionally disabled, psychological disability

Selbstbeherrschung self-control

Selbstbestimmung self-determination

Selbstbeteiligung contributory payment, patient's contributions

Selbstbewusstsein self-confidence, self-consciousness

Selbsteinschätzung self-appraisal, self-image

Selbsterfahrung self-perception

Selbstfindung self-realization, self perception, self cognisance

Selbsthilfe self-help

Selbsthilfefirmen self-help enterprises

Selbsthilfegruppe self-help, mutual aid group

Selbsthilfeverbände self-help organizations

Selbstkonzepte self-constructs

Selbstmord suicide

Selbstmordversuch attempted suicide

selbstständig independent, freelance

Selbstschädigung self-harm

Selbstverwaltung (Gemeinden) autonomy, self-administration

Selbstverwaltung (Körperschaft) self-government

Selbstverwaltung (Versicherungen) (soz.) self-management

Selbstwertgefühl self-esteem

Senior/in senior citizen, elderly

Seniorenklub senior citizen's club

Seniorenzentrum senior citizen's centre

sensibel sensitive

Seuche epidemic

Sexualerziehung sex education

sexueller Missbrauch (von Kindern etc.) sexual abuse (of children etc.)

Sicherheit security, safety

Sicherheit, soziale social security

Sicherheitsmassnahme safety precaution

Sicherungsverwahrung protective custody, detention

Siedlung settlement, (housing, residental) estate

Sinn meaning, mind

Sinnesbehinderung impaired sensory function, sensory disablment

Sinnesänderung change of mind

sinnlos meaningless, pointless, without point

Sinti gipsies

Sitte custom

sittenwidrig immoral

Situationsbericht report on the situation

sitzenbleiben to have to repeat a year

Sitzung meeting

Sitzungsperiode session, term

Sitzungszimmer conference room

Skala scale, range

Soforthilfe emergency relief

Solidargemeinschaft collective community of the insured

Solidarität solidarity

Sollvorschrift (jur.) directory provisions

Sonderfall special case

Sonderkindergarten remedial, special nursery

Sonderschule (päd.) school for physically, mentally or emotionally handicapped children, remedial school, special school (UK)

Sonderpädagogik therapeutic education

Sonderregelung special arrangement, special rules

Sorge, Ärger worry, trouble

Sorge, Fürsorge care

sorgeberechtigt to have custody (right)

Sorgerecht (elterliches) (jun.) (parental) right to custody (für, of)

Sorgerechtsentscheidung custody order

sorgfältig careful, thorough

Sozialabgaben (Sozialbeiträge) social contributions

Sozialamt (D) local social services department (UK), public welfare, public assistance office (USA)

Sozialarbeit social work, welfare work 🕮 social intervention

Sozialarbeit, allgemeine generic social work

Sozialarbeit, aufsuchende outreach work

Sozialarbeit, betriebliche industrial, occupational social work

Sozialarbeit, im Gesundheitswesen medical social work

Sozialarbeit, im Krankenhaus hospital social work

Sozialarbeit, im Strafvollzug social work in penal institutions

Sozialarbeit, in der Psychiatrie psychiatric social work

Sozialarbeiter/in social worker 🕮 social intervention

Sozialatlas social map, chart

Sozialausgaben social expenditure

Sozialberater/in für ausländische Arbeitnehmer (D) advice worker for migrant workers

Sozialberichterstattung social accounting (Government)

Sozialbindung social obligation

Sozialbudget (Europäische Gemeinschaft) Social Budget (expenditure in member countries)

Sozialdienst, Allgemeiner (ASD) general social service

Sozialdienste, besondere (BSD) specialised social services

soziale Arbeit social work, welfare work 🕮 social intervention

soziale Berufe social service professions, caring, helping professions

soziale Daseinsvorsorge general social provision

soziale Einrichtungen social provisions, social service agencies

soziale Gerechtigkeit social justice

soziale Infrastruktur social infrastructure, infrastructure of welfare services

soziale Kompetenz social competence, coping socially

soziale Kontrolle social control

soziale Sicherheit social security

sozialer Brennpunkt socially deprived area, disadvantaged area

sozialer Dienst social service

sozialer Schutz social protection

sozialer Wandel social change, development, transformation, transmutation

soziales Netz social net, "net" of social security

Sozialfonds social fund

Sozialgeheimnis (D) official secrecy in welfare work

Sozialgericht social court

Sozialgesetzbuch social code

Sozialhilfe social, public assistance, social welfare, welfare assistance

Sozialrichtlinien guide-lines for the implementation of social assistance law

Sozialstatistik statistics on social assistance

Sozialtourismus social tourism, welfare tourism

Sozialträger agencies of social assistance

Sozialindikator social indicator

Sozialisation socialisation

Sozialisationshilfen assistance towards socialisation

Sozialleistungen benefits, social provisions

Sozialleistungsempfänger/in social welfare recipients, benefit recipient, people on welfare

Sozialleistungsträger, öffentliche public welfare agencies

Sozialmedizin community medicine

Sozialmediziner/in physician specialising in community medicine, sociomedical doctor

Sozialordnung social order, social system 🕮 Sozialstaat

Sozialpädagoge/Sozialpädagogin social pedagogue, social worker

Sozialpädogogik social pedagogics

Sozialpädiatrie social paediatrics

sozialpädiatrisches Zentrum (behinderte Kinder) (D) socialpaediatric centre

sozialpflegerische Dienste (D) personal social welfare and inhome nursing services

Sozialplan social compensation plan (in the case of a change in operations)

Sozialplanung social planning

Sozialpolitik social policy, social administration

Sozialprodukt (Brutto-, Netto-) national product (gross, net)

Sozialpsychiatrie community psychiatry

sozialpsychiatrischer Dienst community psychiatric service

Sozialpsychologie social psychology

Sozialraum social setting, social space

Sozialraumorientierung orientation on the social space

Sozialrecht welfare law, social law

Sozialreform social reform

Sozialstaat welfare state 🕮 Sozialstaat

Sozialstaatsklausel (im Grundgesetz) (D) Welfate State Clause (in the constitution)

Sozialstation social centre

Sozialstruktur social structure

Sozialsystem social system, societal order, political Order 🕮 Sozialstaat

sozialtherapeutische Anstalt centre for social rehabilitation (penal institution)

Sozialtherapie social therapy, treatment

Sozialtherapeut/in social therapist

Sozialurlaub (Strafvollzug, Resozialisation oder Notfall in der Familie) temporary release from prison on social grounds

Sozialverhalten social behaviour

Sozialversicherung social insurance, security, National Insurance (UK)

Sozialverwaltung (Institution), (Lehrgebiet) social welfare administration, social administration, social welfare authorities

Sozialwesen social affairs, social system

Sozialwissenschaften social sciences

Sozialwohnungen council housing, council dwelling

Soziologe sociologist

Soziologie sociology

Spätaussiedler late resettlers

Spätentwickler/in retarded child

Spätwirkung delayed effect

Spaltung split, disruption

Sparmassnahme economy measure, cut-back

Sparpolitik cost-cutting policy, cost-cutting measures

Sparsamkeit thrift, economy, (strikte) austerity, (Geiz) parsimony

Sparzulage saving bonus

Spende donation

Spender (med., soz.) donor

Sperrgebiet prohinited area

Sperrvermerk restricted notice

Sperrzeit period of exclusion from benefit

Spezialausbildung specialised training

Spezialfach special subject

Spezialfall special case

Spezialgebiet special topic

Spiel game, match

Spielautomat gambling machine

Spielgefährte playmate

Spielsucht compulsory gambling

Spieltherapie play therapy

Spielzeug toy

Spital (A) ⇒ Krankenhaus

Sprachbarriere language barrier

Sprachbehinderung speech impediment

Spracherwerb language aquisition

sprachlos speechless

Spruchstellen (für Fürsorgestreitigkeiten) (D) arbitration boards between agencies of social assistance (FRG)

staatlicher Bereich statutory sector

Staatsangehörigkeit nationality, citizenship

Staatsausgaben public spending

Staatsgewalt state (or public) authority

Staatsverschuldung national debt

Stabssystem (adm.) staff system

Städtebauförderung urban development scheme

Städteplanung urban development

Stadtjugendamt municipal youth office

Stadtkämmerer city treasurer

Stadtrandsiedlung suburban estate

Stadtstreicher city tramp, vagrant people

Stadtstreicherin bag lady (USA)

Stadtteil urban district

Stadtteilarbeit (soz.) community work, patch social work (combination of services within an area)

Stadtverwaltung local administration

Stammbelegschaft primary labour force

Standesamt registrar's office

Standesbewusstsein status, consciousness of status

Starthilfe initial help, start-up money, pumping

priming

stationär in-patient, institutional, stationary

stationär (med., Fall) in-patient, (med., soz.) institutional (services, treatment, provisions)

Stellenangebot job offer

Stellenausschreibung job advertisment

Stellenbechreibung job discription

Sterbebegleitung palliative care, hospice care, care of the dying

Sterbegeld death grant, death benefit

Sterbehilfe palliative care, euthanasia

Sterbeklinik hopice

Sterbepflege ⇒ Sterbebegleitung

Sterblichkeit mortality

stetig steady

Stetigkeit steadiness, constancy, continuity

Steuerausgleich tax equalisation

Steuerbefreiung tax exemption

steuerbegünstigt tax-deductible

Steuerbescheid taxt assessment

Steuererklärung tax return

Steuererstattung tax rebate

steuerfrei tax-free

Steuerfreibetrag tax-free allowance

Steuerfreiheit tax exemption

Steuerlast tax bruden

Steuerpflicht liability to tax

Steuerpolitik taxation policy

Steuerregression progressive taxation

Steuerungsmodelle, neue new directive models

Stichwort keyword, headword, buzzword

Stiefeltern step parents

Stiefkind step child

Stiftung (Organisationsform) foundation

Stiftung (Schenkung) endowment, donation

Stimmabgabe vote, voting

Stimmenthaltung abstention

Stipendium studentship, grant, scholarship, fellowship

Stipendium (CH) ⇒ Ausbildungsförderung

stören disturb

Störung disturbance

stolz proud, (noun) pride

Strafaufschub reprieve

Strafaussetzung (zur Bewährung) suspension of sentence

strafbar punishable

Strafe punishment, penalty, sentence

Strafentlassene/r released prisoner, ex-convict

Strafentlassener, bedingt prisoner on parole, parolee

Straffälligenhilfe probation, assistance to delinquents and their families, welfare work with delinquents

straffrei unpunished

Strafgefangene, Hilfe für (soz.) prison welfare

Strafgerichtsbarkeit jurisdiction

Strafgesetzbuch penal code

strafmildernd mitigating

strafmündig responsible age

Strafmündigkeit age of criminal responsibility

Strafprozess criminal procedure, trial

Strafprozessordnung code of criminal procedure

Strafrecht (als Wissenschaft) penology, criminology

Strafrecht (Summe der Gesetze) criminal, penal law

Strafprozess criminal proceeding, criminal case, trial

Strafrecht criminal law

strafrechtliche Verantwortlichkeit criminal responsibility

Strafrechtspflege criminal, penal justice

Strafregister police record

Strafregister (des Einzelnen) criminal record

Straftat criminal offence

Strafverteidiger defence counsel, defence lawyer

Strafvollzug execution of sentence, prison methods

Strafvollzug, geschlossener imprisonment

Strafvollzug, offener execution of sentence in an open unit or from home

Straßensänger/in busker

Straßensozialarbeit street (corner) work, detached social and youth work, outreach work

Streifendienst patrol on duty

Streik strike

Streik, wilder wildcat strike

Streit quarrel, argument, handgreiflich: brawl, fight

Strich, auf den ~ gehen walk the streets, solicit

Stricher male prostitute

strittig controversial

Studienabschluss degree, diploma

stückweise piecemeal, incremental

Stundung deferment of payment, respite, period of grace

Subkultur subculture

Subsidiarität subsidiarity
Subsidiarität

Sucht addiction

substanziell essential, fundamental

suchterzeugend addictive

Suchtgefährdete/r problem user (of drugs), problem drinker

Suchtkranke/r sufferer from an addiction

Suchtkriminalität drug-related crime

Suchtmittel addictive substance, narcotic,

Suchtmittelabhängigkeit drug dependence

süchtig addicted

Süchtige/r addict, dependent

Suchtkranke/r addict

Suchtkriminalität drug-related crime

Suchtstoff narcotics, dope

suggestiv suggestive

Supervision supervision

Supervisor/in supervisor

sympathisch likeable, nice, pleasant

– T –

Tabelle table

tabuisieren taboo

Tageseinrichtungen day facilities, day care centres

Tagesheim nursery

Tagesstätte (Tagesförderstätte) für schwerstbehinderte Jugendliche und Erwachsene (D) day care and rehabilitation centre for most severely handicapped (disabled) young people and adults

Tagesklinik (psych.) day hospital

Tagesmutter (D) child minder (registered)

Tagespflege day care

Tagespflegestätte day care centre

Tagestaxe (CH) – Pflegesatz

talentiert talented, gifted

Tarifeinkommen Agreed Wages and Saleries

Tarifvertrag wage agreement

Taschendieb pickpocket

Taschengeld pocket money

Tatbestand facts, factual situation

Täter/in perpetrator

Tätigkeit activity

tätlich violent

Tatsachenbericht documentary

tatsächlich real, actual, in fact

tatsächlicher Aufenthalt actual place of residence

Tatverdacht suspicion

taub deaf

Taubheit deafness

taubstumm deaf-mute

Taubstummensprache sign language, manual alphabet (language), finger alphabet (language) 📖 sign language

Taufe baptism, christening

täuschen deceive

Täuschung deception

Tauschwirtschaft barter economy, subsistence economy

Teestube drop-in centre

teilen share devide

Teilnahmeberechtigung eligibility

Teilnahmebescheinigung certificate of attendance

teilnahmslos indifferent

teilnehmen participate, take part

Teilnehmer/in participant

Teilrente partial pension

Teilzeitarbeit part-time work

Telefonhilfen help-line

Telefonkette (sen.) telephone reassurance

Telefonseelsorge telephone emergency service, help line, Samaritans (Organisation, die diesen Dienst anbietet)

Thema subject, topic, issue

Therapeut/in therapist

therapeutische Gemeinschaft therapteutic community

therapeutische Wohngemeinschaft therapeutic community (group living)

therapeutisches Team therapeutic team

Tiefenpsychologie depth psychology

Tischvorlage briefing document, discussion document

Todesfall death, (in der Familie) bereavement, (Todesfall, aber auch Verletzte) casualty

Todesstrafe death penalty

todkrank terminal ill

Totschlag manslaughter

totale Institution total, closed institution

Träger agency, body, organisation

trägerübergreifend jointly organised

Training, soziales (bes. junge Rechtsbrecher) social skills training (esp. course for juvenile delinquents)

Trauer grief, mourning, sorrow

Trauerfeier funeral service

trauern mourn

Trebegänger/in (veraltet) juvenile tramp, homelsss young person

Treffpunkt meeting place

Trennung von Tisch und Bett separation from bed and board

Trinker/in heavy drinker, alcoholic

Trost consolation, comfort

trostlos hopeless

Trotz defiance

trotzig defiant

Trübsinn gloom, melancholy

Trümmerfrauen (D) (lit.) "rubble women"

Trunksucht problem drinking, alcohol addiction, alcoholism, dipsomania

– U –

Übelkeit nausea

Überalterung aging

Überbau superstructure

überbelegt (Wohnung, Heim) overcrowded

Überbrückungshilfe interim aid

Überbrückungskredit bridging loan

Übereinstimmung agreement, correspondence, conformity

überempfindlich oversensitive

Übergangsbestimmung transitory regulation, transitory disposition

Übergangseinrichtung halfway house, transitional home

Übergangsgeld transition payment

Übergangsheim (soz.) halfway house, hostel, transitory home

übergangsweise transitional

übergreifen spill-over

überheblich arrogant

Überlastung strain, stress

überlegen superior, think something over

Überleitung (Ansprüche) transfer (of claims)

Übermaß excess

Übermüdung overtiredness

Übernachtung overnight stay

überörtlich regional

überörtlicher Träger (der Sozialhilfe) regional agency (of public assistance)

Überprüfung (Unterlagen, Fall) review, reappraisal

Überschuldung excessive indebtedness

Übertretung (jur.) transgression

überzeugen coax

Überzeugung conviction

Umerziehung re-education

Umfeld environment

Umgebung (Hintergrund, Konstellation) setting, (räumlich) surroundings

Umorganisation reorganisation

Umschulung retraining

unanfechtbar incontestable

unanständig rude

unausgeglichen unbalanced, unstable

unbefugt unauthorized

unbegründet unfounded

unbeholfen awkward

unentgeltliche Beförderung Schwerbehinderter free transport for severely disabled people

Unfall accident, casualty

Unfallopfer casualty

Unfallrente accident pension

Unfallschutz accident protection, safety at work

Unfallverhütung prevention of accidents

Unfallversicherung, gesetzliche statutory accident insurance

ungeschickt awkward

ungültig invalid

ungünstig adverse

Unterbringung (von Personen) placement

unterentwickelt underdeveloped

Unterhalt (Ehegatten-) maintenance, alimony (Kinder) child support

Unterhaltsgeld (Arbeitsamt) maintenance allowance

Unterhaltshilfe (soz.) maintenance assistance

Unterhaltspflicht maintenance responsibility

Unterhaltssicherung (Wehrdienstleistende) (D) safeguarding of the subsistence of servicemen and their dependents

Unterhaltsvorschuss maintenance advance

Unterhaltszahlung maintenance payment

Unterhaltszuschuss subsistence allowance

Unterkunft (generell) housing, accommodation

Unterkunft (Notunterkunft) (emergency) shelter

Unterkunftskosten actual cost of accommodation (public assistance benefit)

Unterstützung relief, support

Untersuchung (jur.) investigation

Untersuchung (med.) inspection, examination

Untersuchung (psych.) exploration

Untersuchungshaft (jur.) remand, custody, detention (awaiting trial)

Untersuchungshaftanstalt remand prison

unwirtschaftlich(es Verhalten) uneconomical, wasteful (behaviour)

Unzucht mit Kindern, Abhängigen sexual abuse of children, dependents

Unzufriedenheit, soziale social discontent

Unzurechnungsfähigkeit ⇒ Zurechnungsunfähigkeit

Urkunde document, instrument, deed

Urlaub ⇒ leave, holiday, vacation

Ursprungsfamilie family of origin

Urteil judgement

Urteil, gerichtliches court decision, order

– V –

Vater father

Vaterschaft paternity

Vaterschaftsanerkennung acknowlegement of paternity

Vaterschaftsfeststellung ascertainment of paternity

Vaterschaftsprozess paternity trial, affiliation proceedings (UK), paternity suit (USA)

Veranlagung (psych.) predisposition, natural propensity

Verarmung (Vorgang) impoverishment

Verarmung (Zustand) destitution

Verband, freier private association

Verband, international non-governmental organisation (NGO)

Verbraucherberatung consumer advice

verbrecherisch criminal

Verbürgerlichung embourgeoisement

Verbund, Versorgungs~ combine, interlocking system

Verdacht suspicion

verdeckte Arbeitslosigkeit hidden unmeployment

Verdrängung (psych.) repression

Verein association

Vereinsrecht law of associations

Vereinbarkeit (Vorschriften, Maßnahmen, Ziele) compatibility

Vereinbarkeit von Beruf und Familie family friendliness

Vereinigungsfreiheit freedom of association

Vereinsamung isolation

Vereinspflegschaft (auch: Vereinsvormundschaft) curatorship, guardianship, trusteeship by an association

Verfahren procedure

Verfahrensangleichung adjustment of procedure(s)

Verfassung (Grundgesetz) (D) constitution, basic law

Verfassungsänderung ammendement of the constitution

Verfassungsgericht constitutional court

Verfassungsrecht constitutional law

verfassungswidrig unconstitutional

Verfügung (jur.) decree, administrative order Verfügungsbefugnis right of disposal

Verführung Minderjähriger sexual interference with a minor

Vergehen offense

Vergeltung retaliation

Vergeltungsmassnahme reprisal

Vergewaltigung (forcible) rape, sexual abuse

Vergleich (jur.) settlement

Vergünstigung fringe benefits

Verhalten behaviour

Verhaltensauffälligkeit deviant, unusual behaviour

Verhaltensforschung behavioural science, research

verhaltensgestört, schwierig maladjusted

Verhaltensprobleme conduct problems

Verhaltenspsychologie behaviourism

Verhaltensstörung conduct disorder

Verhaltenstherapie behaviour modification

Verhaltensweise pattern of behaviour

Verhältnismäßigkeit, Grundsatz der principle of (being reasonable and) proportionality 🕮 Subsidiarität

Verhinderung prevention

Verhör interrogation, inquiry

Verjährung limitation

Verjährungsfrist period of limitation

Verknüpfung, organisatorische linkup

Verlegenheit embarrassemant

Verlegenheitslösung stopgap

Verletzbarkeit vulnaribility

Verletztengeld injury benefit

Verletztenrente injury pension

Verletzung injury

verleugnen deny

verleumden slander, libel

verlieren lose

verlockend tempting

Verlust forfeiture, loss, (Todesfall, Verletzte) casualty, (Todesfall) death, (in der Familie) bereavement

Vermächtnis legacy

Vermarktung marketing

Vermieter landlord, lessor

Vermieterin landlady, lessor

Vermittlung (Heim, Pflegeheim) (sen.) referral (Streitigkeit) mediation

Vermögen (Geldwert) assets (Leistungsfähigkeit) ability

Vermögensbildung formation of assets

Vermögensfreigrenze (soz.) ⇒ Schonvermögen

Vermögenssorge ⇒ Pflegschaft

Vernachlässigung neglect

Vernehmung hearing, interrogation

Vernetzung networking, linking-up

Verordnung (jur.) decree, ordinance, order

Verordnung (med.) prescription

Verpflichtung obligation, commitment, engagement

Verrechtlichung increasing legal influence

verrückt crazy, mad, insane

Versäumnis failing, default

verschämt bashful, coy

verschieden different

Verschlechterung worsening, deterioration

Verschleppung abduction

Verschlüsselung coding

Verschollene/r missing, untraceable person

Verschuldung indebtedness

Verschwiegenheit ⇒ Schweigepflicht

Versehrte (A) ⇒ Behinderte

verselbstständigen becoming independent, getting independent

Versicherung insurance

Versicherungsamt statutory insurance supervision authority

Versicherungsberechtigung eligibility for insurance

Versicherungsgesellschaft insurance agency, insurance company

Versicherungspflicht obligatory insurance

Versorgung (med.) medical care, attendance

Versorgung (s.S.) maintenance, pension

Versorgung (stationär, ambulant) care, services

Versorgungsamt (insbes. Kriegsopfer) war pension, maintenance office

Versorgungsausgleich (Ehescheidung) splitting of pension rights on divorce

Versorgungskrankengeld (D) special sickness benefit for war victims and severely disabled people

versprechen pledge

Verstoß (gegen Vorschrift, Gesetz, Vereinbarung) violation (of rule, law, agreement), infringement

Vertrag (privatechtlich) contract, agreement

Vertrag (staatsrechtlich) treaty, convention

Vertragsstrafe contractual fine

Vertrauensarzt medical examiner (appointed by insurance company, welfare agency, etc.)

Vertrauensmann (für Schwerbehinderte im Betrieb) special representative of disabled employees

Vertriebene (allg.) Aussiedler

Vertriebenenrente (D) pensions for displaced and expelled or resettled Germans and their dependents

Vertriebenenverbände (D) associations of expellees (resettled Germans)

vertuschen gloss over

Verursachung causation

Verurteilung conviction

verwahrlost (veraltet) neglected, abandoned, destitute

Verwahrlosung (Erwachsene) social maladjustement

Verwahrlosung (Kinder) neglect

verwalten manage, administer

Verwaltung (Dienststelle) administration

Verwaltung (Staatsgewalt, im Sinne der Gewaltenteilung) executive (as opposed to legislation, judiciary)

Verwaltungsakt administrative act

Verwaltungsgericht Administrative Court

Verwaltungsgerichtsbarkeit administrative jurisdiction

Verwaltungsprozess (jur.) trial in an administrative court

Verwaltungsrecht administrative law

Verwaltungsverfahren administrative procedure

Verwahrlosung state of destitution, social maldajustment

Verweildauer (Krankenhaus, Pflegeheim) length of stay

Verweildauer, durchschnittliche average length of stay

Verwendung, nachweisen der prove of use

Verwendungsnachweis proof of use

Verwirkung (jur.) forfeiture

Verzeitlichung temporarisation

Verzicht renunciation, relinquishment

Verzichtserklärung (jur.) waiver

Verzug (Fristüberschreitung) delay

Verzug (jur.) default

Volkshochschule further education college, adult evening classes

Volksrente (veraltet) universal pension, demogrant

Volljährigkeit ⇒ Mündigkeit

Vollmacht authority, power of attorney, procuration, proxy

Vollstreckung (jur.) enforcement, execution

Vollstreckungsbescheid writ of execution

Vollstreckungsschutz (⇒ Pfändungsschutz) exemption from execution

Vollstreckung, vorbeugende Hilfe preventative measures

Vorbeugung ⇒ Prävention

Vorfall incident

vorgesetzte Behörde higher authority

Vorgesetzte/r (adm.) superior

Vorladung summons, citation

Vorleistungspflicht obligation to advance money to sb.

Vormund guardian Einzelvormund individual guardian

Vormund (Jugendamt) official guardian (local services department)

Vormundschaft (amtliche) (official) guardianship

Vormundschaft (Vereinsvormundschaft) guardianship (by an association)

Vormundschaft anordnen (v., jur.) issue a care order

Vormundschaftsgericht court dealing with guardianship matters

Vormundschaftshilfe guardianship court assistance

Vorrang (Gesetz, Leistungspflicht) precedence, primacy, priority

Vorruhestandsgeld pre-retirement benefit

Vorschrift disposition, regulation

Vorschule pre-school

Vorschuss advance payment

Vorsorge (Prävention) prevention, prophylaxis

Vorsorge (Zukunfts~, Daseins~) provident provision

Vorsorgeuntersuchung preventative health check

Vorstand board, executive committee

Vorstrafe previous conviction

Vorurteil prejudice, label

– W –

Wachstum growth

Wachstumshemmung inhibition of growth

Währung currency

Währungssystem monetary system

wahlberechtigt entitled to vote

Wahlfach optional subject

Wahlkampagne veranstalten canvass

Wahrnehmung apperception, cognition, perception

Wahrnehmung, soziale social perception

Wahrung (Grundsatz, Vorschrift) adherence to sth.

Wahrung (Interessen des Klienten) protection (of client interests)

Wahrung (Rechte) respect of rights

Waise orphan

Waisenrente orphan's benefits

Wandel change, shift, transformation

Wandel von Auffassungen, Einstellungen attitudinal shift

Wandel, durchgreifender transformation, transmutation

Wandel, gesellschaftlicher social change

Wanderung migration

Wanderungssaldo balance of migration

Ware commodity, product, merchandise

Warenkorb (soz.) bread basket, shopping, market basket (measure to determine cost of living fluctuations, in social assistance to determine the subsistence level)

Warnstreik token strike

Wartezeit (s.S.) waiting period

Wartung ⇒ Pflege

Wehrdienst military service

Wehrdienstverletzung injury incurred during military service

Wehrdienstverweigerer conscientious objector

Wehrschutz (CH) ⇒ Wehrdienst

Weisung directive, instruction

Weisung zur Betreuung (jur.) supervision order

Weisungsbefugnis authority to issue directives

Weiterbildung further education

Werkstatt für Behinderte sheltered workshop

Wettbewerb competition, contest

widerrechtlich illegal, unlawful

Widerruf revocation, withdrawal

Widerspruch einlegen, erheben (v.) protest, object to sth.

widrig adverse

Wiederaufnahmeverfahren reopening of a case

Wiedereingliederung rehabilitation

Wiedergutmachung restitution of assets and rights

wirtschaftlich economic, economical

wirtschaftlich aktive Person engaged in economic activity

Wirtschaftlichkeit (einer Maßnahme) economic efficiency

Wirtschaftsflüchtling (abwertend) economically motivated asylum applicant

Witwengeld widow's allowance

Witwenrente widow's pension

Witwerrente widower's pension

Wohlfahrtspflege, freie non-statutory welfare

Wohlfahrtspflege, Spitzenverbände der freien central voluntary welfare organizations

Wohlfahrtsstaat welfare state 📖 Sozialstaat

Wohlfahrtsverband welfare association, welfare organisation, charity 📖 Wohlfahrtsverband

wohltätig charitable, benevolent

Wohltätigkeitsverein charity (UK), humanity (USA)

Wohngeld housing benefit, allowance

Wohngemeinschaft housing community, communal living, group quarters, commune, group residence (USA)

Wohngruppe, therapeutische therapeutic group home

Wohnheim supervised housing, hostel, dormitory, rooming house

Wohnsiedlung housing estate

Wohnsitz place (of domicile), residence, abode

Wohnsitz, ohne festen without fixed abode

Wohnumfeld habitat

Wohnung accommodation, dwelling, flat (UK), apartment (USA)

Wohnung, behindertengerechte adapted housing, accommodation (UK), mobility housing (USA)

Wohnungsamt housing office, housing department (UK), public housing agency (USA)

Wohnungsbau, sozialer council housing (UK), public housing (USA), social housing

Wohnungsbaugenossenschaft housing association

Wohnungsloser, alleinstehender homeless single (unattached) person

Wohnungswesen housing

Wohnverhältnisse, mangelhafte substandard housing

Wunsch- und Wahlrecht (soz., jun.) right to express preferences (D)

– X –

Xenophobie xeanophobia

– Z –

Zahlung payment

Zahlungsbilanz balance of payments

Zahlungsverzug overdue payment

Zeichnungsbefugnis authority to sign

Zeitarbeit temporary work

Zeugnis (Aussage) (jur.) evidence, testimony

Zeugnis (Beruf) reference

Zeugnis (Schule) report, certificate

Zeugnisverweigerungsrecht right to refuse giving evidence

Ziel (Absicht) aim, (Zielpunkt) goal, (Focus) objective, (Soll) target

Zielgruppe target group

Zigeuner (veraltet) gipsy, Sinti, Roma

Zins interest

Zinssatz interest rate

Zivildienst compulsory non-military national service, civilian service by conscientious objectors

Zivildienstleistender non-military serviceman

Zivilgericht civil court

Zivilprozess civil suit, action

Zivilrecht civil law, private law

Zuchthaus (veraltet) (D) penitentiary (obsolete)

Zuchtmittel (Jugendstrafrecht) corrective measures

zügeln curb

Zugang access

Zugewinngemeinschaft (Eherecht) statutory property regime of the community of surplus (despite its name: a separation of property with equalization of the goods. Acquired during marriage)

Zuhälter procurer, pander

Zulage supplementary benefits

Zulassungsbedingung condition of admission

Zukunftskonferenz future search conference

Zulage supplementary allowance

Zumutbarkeit reasonableness

Zurechnungsfähigkeit, verminderte (jur.), diminished responsibility

Zurechnungsunfähigkeit (jur.) being not criminally responsible

Zusage (jur.) promise, (Einwilligung) assent, consent, (Einladung) acceptance,

Zusatzurlaub für Schwerbehinderte Additional annual leave for severely disabled people

Zusatzversicherung supplementary insurance

Zusatzversorgung supplementary pension

Zuschuss subsidy, subvention, contribution

Zusprechen eines Kindes (bei der Scheidung) (jur.) grant sb. Custody of a child.

zuständig competent, relevant, responsible

Zuständigkeit(sbereich)(adm.) (area of) competence, responsibility, jurisdiction

Zuständigkeit, sachliche subject matter jurisdiction, departmental responsibility

Zuteilung (Lebensmittel) apportionment (Wohnung) allocation

Zuweisung (Aufgabe) asignment

Zuweisung (Mittel, Arbeitsplätze) allocation

Zuwendung (Geldmittel) (adm.) grant-in-aid

Zuwendung (psych.) affection, nurture (USA)

Zuwendungsbescheid notice of grant (or allowance)

Zwang compulsion, (Erzwingung) coercion

Zwang (psych.) obsession

Zwangsarbeit forced labour

Zwangseinweisung compulsory/involuntary admission/detention (in a psychiatric hospital)

Zwangsgeld (jur.) compulsory enforced payment

Zwangslage predicament

Zwangsmaßnahme compulsory measure

Zwangsmittel (jur.) coercive measures, enforcement by law

Zwangsneurose obsessional neurosis

Zwangsräumung (jur.) eviction

Zwangsversteigerung auction ordered by the court

Zwangsvollstreckung coercive seizure, distraint execution, execution proceedings

Zweck purpose

zweckgebunden (Leistung, Zuwendung) earmarked (payment, grant), granted for a specific purpose

Zweigstelle branch (office)

English – German

– A –

abandon verlassen, vernachlässigen

ability Fähigkeit, Befähigung

ability test Eignungstest

abnormal anomal, anormal

abortion Schwangerschaftsabbruch

abstinence Abstinenz

abuse Missbrauch, Misshandlung, missbrauchen, misshandeln

abuse of office Amtsmissbrauch

abused and abandoned children misshandelte und vernachlässigte Kinder

acceptance Akzeptanz, Annahme, Billigung

access Zugang

accessibility Erreichbarkeit

accession Beitritt

accident Unfall

accident prevention Unfallverhütung

accident protection Unfallschutz

accommodate unterbringen, anpassen

accommodation Anpassung (an soziale Umstände, Abfinden mit sozialen Umständen), Schlichtung, Unterkunft

accountability Zurechenbarkeit, Verantwortlichkeit, Zuordenbarkeit von Verantwortung

accountant Buchhalter/in

accounts Konten

accredit bestätigen

accreditation Bestätigung

acculturation Akkulturation, kulturelle Anpassung, kulturelle Angleichung

achievement society Leistungsgesellschaft

acknowledgement Anerkennung (Anspruch, Examen)

acknowledgement of paternity Vaterschaftsanerkennung

act Gesetz, Urkunde, Verfügung, Akte

action research Handlungsforschung

activating care aktivierende Pflege

activist Aktivist, Aktiver, Tätiger, Engagierter

activity therapy Aktivitätstherapie

activity-theory Aktivitätstheorie

adaptation Anpassung

adapted housing, adapted accommodation (UK) behindertengerechte Wohnung

adbusting gezielte Änderung der Aussage von Plakatwerbung durch Hinzufügen von Aussagen, Überkleben von Teilen etc. mit politischem Anspruch

addict Süchtige/r

addictive suchterzeugend (sowohl in verhaltensmäßiger Sicht [addictive behaviour] als auch in stofflicher Hinsicht [addictive substance – Suchtmittel]

additional benefit Mehrleistung (z.B. Krankenkasse), Zusatzleistung

additional payment zusätzliche Zahlung, Nachzahlung

additional allowance aufstockende Leistung

additionality Zusätzlichkeit

adherence Einhaltung, Wahrung (Vorschrift)

adjudication Entscheidung, Urteil

adjustement Anpassung, Angleichung

administration Verwaltung, Leitung (Dienststelle)

administration of justice Rechtspflege

administrative court Verwaltungsgericht

administrative law Verwaltungsrecht

administrative machinery Verwaltungsapparat

administrative regulation Verwaltungsvorschrift

administrative ruling Verwaltungsverfügung

admission ward Aufnahmestation (med.)

adolescence Adoleszenz, Jugend

adolescent Heranwachsende/r, Jugendlich(e/r), jugendlich, heranwachsend

adopted order Adoptionsbeschluss

adoption Adoption

adoption officer Mitarbeiter des Sozialamtes (UK), der Jugendbehörde (USA)

adoptive parents Adoptiveltern

adult home (USA) Wohnheim für Erwachsene (mit Minimalversorgung)

adventure playground Abenteuerspielplatz**adverse** widrig, ungünstig, nachteilig

advice Beratung ⇒ consultancy

advise beraten ⇒ consulting

advisory board Beratungsausschuss

advisory committee Beratungsausschuss

advocacy Parteinahme, politische Interessenvertretung

advocate Befürworter, Anwalt, Interessenvertreter – der Begriff wird auch verwendet für Lobbyisten im weiteren Verständnis, also Personen, die als politische Interessenvertreter agieren, ohne dazu parlamentarisch oder vereinsrechtlich bestimmt zu sein ⇒ solicitor ⇒ barrister

affection Zuneigung, Zuwendung (psych.), auch: Gebrechen, Leiden (med.)

affidavit (schriftliche) eidliche Erklärung

affliction Niedergeschlagenheit, Verstimmung (psych.), geistige Beeinträchtigung (med.)

affluence Überfluss, Wohlstand

aftercare Nachbehandlung (med., psych.), nachgehende Sorge (soz.)

age alt werden, altern, Alter

age of discretion Strafmündigkeit

ageism Diskriminierung auf Grund des Alters

agency Organisation, Träger, Dienststelle, Geschäftsstelle, Amt, Zweigstelle

agenda Tagesordnung – auch im übertragenen Sinn, be high on the agenda obenan *od.* ganz oben auf der Tagesordnung stehen, have a hidden agenda heimliche Absichten hegen

agenda setting Bestimmung über die politische Tagesordnung

agent Handelnde/r (im institutionellen Sinn, zu unterscheiden vom *actor* als Person, Individuum)

aggression Aggression

aggressive behaviour Aggressionsverhalten

aging altern (biographisch, demographisch)

agitator Agitator, Aufklärer, Hetzer

agreement Übereinstimmung, Vereinbarung

aid Hilfe

Aid to Families with Dependent Children (AFDC) (USA) Familienhilfe (wichtigstes Sozialhilfeprogramm, überwiegend für vaterlose Familien)

alcohol addict Alkoholsüchtiger

alcohol addiction Trunksucht

alcohol dependency Alkoholabhängigkeit

alcoholism Alkoholismus

alien fremd, Fremder 🕮 Ausländer

alienation Entfremdung

alienist (USA) Psychiater/in (bes. jur.)

alimony Unterhalt (Ehefrau) (jur.)

allocation Zuteilung, Zuweisung

allowance Beihilfe, Bewilligung, Mietbeihilfe, zumeist rent allowance

almoning (obsolete) (UK) ⇒ hospital social work

alternative Alternative, alternativer Weg, alternative Handlung

amendment Änderung, Anpassung, Zusatz (jur.)

amenity Annehmlichkeit, Attraktivität, auch in Verbindung mit anderen Begriffen verwendet, z.B. amenity of residence Wohnqualität

amnesic blackout Bewusstseinslücke (psych.)

anamnesis Anamnese, Vorgeschichte (med., soz.)

anger Wut, Ärger, Zorn

anger management innere Kontrolle von Wutausbrüchen, Selbstbeherrschung

animateur jemand, der Wandel oder allgemein zielgerichtetes Handeln für andere ermöglicht, ohne selbst direkt betroffen sein, d.h. ohne dass dieses Handeln persönliches Handeln ist oder den persönlichen Interessen unmittelbar entsprechen muss, 🕮 social intervention

animation soziokulturelle Arbeit 🕮 social intervention

annoyance Belästigung

annulment Nichtigkeitserklärung

anomalous anomal, anormal

anomic abweichend

anomie Abweichung, Normlosigkeit

anormal (USA) anomal, anormal

apperception Wahrnehmung, Aufmerksamkeit

appliance Hilfsmittel (Geräte) (med.)

applicant Antragsteller/in

application Antrag

appraisal Bewertung, Beurteilung

apprehend (v.) festnehmen, begreifen

apprentice Auszubildende/r

appropriate angemessen

aptitude Fähigkeit(en) (bes. Behinderte)

aptitude test Eignungsprüfung

arbitration Schlichtungsverfahren

architect Architekt/in 🕮 architecture

architecture Architektur 🕮 architecture

area planning Raumordnung 🕮 architecture

arrest Verhaftung, Festnahme

artifical limb Prothese (med.)

arts Kunst 🕮 architecture

arts worker "Laienkünstler", für den Kunst ein "Mittel" zur Entwicklung im Rahmen von Gemeinwesenarbeit darstellt 🕮 architecture

ascertainment Feststellung, Ermittlung

ascertainment of paternity Vaterschaftsfestellung

asocial asozial (abwertend)

assailant Angreifer

assessment Einschätzung, Festsetzung, Beurteilung

assessment basis Bemessungsgrundlage

assets Vermögen, persönlicher Besitz (Geldwert)

assignment Abtretung (Forderung), Übertragung, (Rechte), Zuweisung (Aufgabe)

assistance Hilfe, Fürsorge, Beistand, Beihilfe, Unterstützung

association Verein, Vereinigung, Verband 🕮 Gesellschaft

asylum (USA) Pflegeheim, Heim

asylum applicant Asylbewerber

asylum, right of ~ Asylrecht, Asylanspruch

atomised vereinzelt, zersplittert

attachment of earnings Lohnpfändung (aus Unterhaltsklage)

attendance allowance (UK) Pflegegeld (Behinderte)

attendance Anwesenheit (auch: Teilnehmerzahl), Pflege

attendance centre (UK) (Ort für) Freizeitarrest

attitude Verhalten, Einstellung

attitudinal shift Wandel von Auffassungen, Einstellungen

auction ordered by the court Zwangsversteigerung

audit office Rechnungsprüfungsamt (UK), Rechnungshof

audit Rechnungsprüfung, teils auch: Prüfung von Vorgängen, Organisationen, Strukturen u.a.

auditor Rechnungsprüfer/in

authentication Beglaubigung

authority Autorität, auch verwendet zur Bezeichnung offizieller Stellen, z.B. equal opportunity authority als Gleichstellungsbeauftragte(r) [⇒ commissioner]

authorisation Ermächtigung, Bewilligung

authorize bevollmächtigen, genehmigen

awareness Bewusstsein (auch im Sinn des politischen Bewusstseins)

awareness raising Bewusstseinsentwicklung

awkward ungeschickt, unangenehm

– B –

basic freedom Grundfreiheiten

backslide Rückfall (Gewohnheit)

bag lady (USA) Stadtstreicherin

balance Ausgleich, ausgleichen

ban on discrimination Benachteiligungsverbot

barrister Rechtsanwalt/Rechtsanwältin (bei höheren Gerichten)

bashing körperliche Misshandlung

basic (human) rights Grundrechte

basic necessities Lebensgrundlagen

basic needs Grundbedürfnisse (soz.)

basic nursing Grundpflege (med.)

basic wage Grundlohn, Grundgehalt

battered child misshandeltes Kind

battered wives shelter Frauenhaus, more frequently women's refuge

battering Gewalttätigkeit (insb. Ausübung physischer Gewalt gegen Unterlegene) ⇒ domestic violence

bed-wetting Bettnässen

beggar Bettler/in

begging Betteln

behaviour Verhalten

behavioural sciences Verhaltenswissenschaften

behavioural therapy Verhaltenstherapie

behaviourism Verhaltenspsychologie, Lernpsychologie

bother belästigen

benefit (Sozial-)Leistungen, Rente, begünstigen

benevolent wohltätig, wohlwollend

best practice gute Praktiken, gute Beispiele – oft als englischer Begriff weiterverwendet

bias Befangenheit, Neigung (e.g. middle class bias: Ausrichtung an Mittelschichtnormen)

bill Gesetz(esvorlage) 🕮 law

biodiversity biologische Vielfalt in einem Lebensraum

biological family biologische Familie

birth control Geburtenkontrolle

bisexual bisexuell

black economy Schattenwirtschaft, Schwarzarbeit

black labour Schwarzarbeit

blind allowance Blindengeld

board of trustees Kuratorium

boarding home care (USA) einfachste Pensionsunterbringung für Alte, Behinderte usw.

body language Körpersprache

bond Bindung

border Grenze

borderline case Grenzfall

borstal Jugend(straf)anstalt

bottom-up von unten

boundary Begrenzung

braille Braille, Blindenschrift

brainstorm Gedankensammlung

bread-basket Warenkorb (soz.)

breadline Armutsgrenze, Existenzminimum

bread winner Ernährer/in (der Familie), Haushaltsvorstand

bricks and mortar Dach über'm Kopf, Unterbringung, die nicht über das Notwendige hinausgeht, ebenso: Wohnungspolitik, die auf Unterbringung, nicht auf Schaffung von Lebensraum zielt

brief Mandat

briefing Unterrichtung, Einweisung in eine Arbeit, Einführung, Einsatzbesprechung

bring an action klagen (jur.)

building Gebäude, bauen, auch im übertragenen Sinn: building of trust Vertrauensaufbau

bully Rabauke, jemand, der Schwächere schikaniert

bullying schikanieren

business Geschäft, individueller Geschäftsvorgang, Handel, Aufgabe, Betrieb

business plan Geschäftsplan

busker Straßenmusikant/in

buzz Nervenkitzel

buzzword Schlagwort

– C –

campaign Kampagne, Feldzug

campaigner “Kampagnenmanager“

campaigning kämpfen

canvass werben, auch politische Kampagne durchführen, um Stimmen werben

capability Fähigkeit

capable of guilty intent Schuldfähigkeit

capacity Aufnahmefähigkeit, Leistungsfähigkeit

capacity building Förderung der Aufnahmefähigkeit, Leistungsförderung

capacity to work Arbeitsfähigkeit

capital disregard Freibetrag (Sozialhilfe: Vermögen)

care Betreuung, (Für)Sorge, Obhut

care, continuity of ~ durchgehende Hilfe (sen.)

care delivery Betreuungsleistung, Betreuungsdienste

care giver Betreuer/in, auch i.S.v. Bezugsperson

care order Heimeinweisung (Fürsorgeerziehung), gerichtliche Übertragung der Elternrechte auf das Jugendamt (UK)

career Laufbahn, Berufsverlauf

case Fall

case history Fallgeschichte, Vorgeschichte, Krankengeschichte

case management Einzelfallbearbeitung (soz.)

case manager Kontaktperson

case report Fallbericht (soz.)

case study Fallstudie

case work Einzelfallhilfe (soz.) 🕮 social intervention

cash benefit Geldleistung

casual labour Gelegenheitsarbeit

catamnesis Katamnese (nach abgeschlossener Behandlung) (med.,)

category based measure zielbezogene Maßnahme, bei der das Ziel unter dem Gesichtspunkt eines bestimmten Problems gewählt ist, dabei ist eine genaue Abgrenzung zu gruppenbezogenen Maßnahmen nur selten möglich

causation Verursachung

causative verursachend

cede abtreten (einer Forderung)

ceiling Obergrenze, auch Begrenzung (glass ceiling Begrenzung in einem scheinbar für alle Aufstieg gewährenden System (z.B. Bildungssystem, das nach oben für Frauen faktisch nach wie vor schwer zugänglich ist)

central zentral, bedeutsam

centre Gemeindezentrum

centre based work Arbeit an einem bestimmten Ort, dem Gemeindezentrum, Gegenbegriff ⇒ out-reach (work)

cerebral damage Hirnschaden

cerebral palsy frühkindliche Hirnschädigung

certificate of (good) conduct Führungszeugnis, Leumundszeugnis

cession Abtretung (jur.)

chair Vorsitzende/r, Lehrstuhlinhaber/in

chairperson Vorsitzende/r

chamber Kammer (berufsständisch)

champion Fürsprecher, besonders engagierte Person

charge Anzeige (bei der Staatsanwaltschaft), Anklage (jur.)

chargeable anrechnungspflichtig

charitable Wohltätigkeitsorganisation, gemeinnützige Einrichtung

charity 🕮 Wohlfahrtsverband

chart Karte, Diagramm

chemistry Apotheke ⇒ dispensary

child allowance, also children's allowance Kindergeld

child benefits (UK) Kindergeld

child care worker Betreuer/in von Kindern

child education Erziehung (im institutionellen Rahmen)

child guidance clinic Kinder- und Jugendberatungsstelle (heilpädagogisch-psychiatrisch)

child maintenance (UK) private Unterhaltszahlung für Kinder

childminder Kinderbetreuer/in

childminding Kinderbetreuung (außer Haus) ⇒ parenting

child neglect Kindesvernachlässigung

child rearing Kindererziehung

child support Unterhalt für Kinder

child under guardianship Mündel

child welfare department (USA) örtliches oder staatliches Jugendamt

child welfare Jugendfürsorge

child welfare worker Sozialarbeiter/in in der Jugendfürsorge

child abuse Kindesmisshandlung

children exemption (Steuer-Freibetrag für Kinder (USA)

children's day care centre Kindertageseinrichtung, Kindertagsesstätte

children's day home Kindertagesheim

children's home Kinderheim

children's nurse Kinderschwester (med.)

choice Wahl, Auswahl

citizen Bürger/in

citizen's Advice Bureau (UK) Bügerberatungsstelle

citizenry Bürgerschaft

citizenship Staatsbürgerschaft

citizenship, post-nuptial citizenship Bürgerschaft durch Heirat

citizenship by decent Staatsbürgerschaft durch Abstammung

citizenship by naturalisation Einbürgerung

city Stadt

cityscape Stadtumriss, analog zu *landscape,* Landschaft, der Begriff bezieht sich dabei auf cie Umrisse, die Skizze der Stadt und ist damit von Bedeutung für die Darstellung der räumlichen und vor allem baulichen Ausgangslage für gemeindenahe Stadtplanung, -entwicklung und -veränderung

civic-affairs Bürgerangelegenheiten

civic affairs centre Behördenzentrum

civil law Zivilrecht

civil servant Beamter/Beamtin

civil Society Zivilgesellschaft
📖 civil society

civil suit Zivilprozess

civil court Zivilgericht

claim (Rechts-) Anspruch, Forderung, Anspruch erheben, fordern

claimant Antragsteller/in, Anspruchsberechtigte/r, Kläger/in

class specific (upbringing) schichtspezifisch(e) (Erziehung)

client-centred klientenzentriert (psych.)

clientel Klienten, Patienten, Kunden

clientelist klientelistisch

clinical social work (USA) therapeutische Sozialarbeit

clinical-psychology klinische Psychologie

clothing allowance Bekleidungshilfe

cluster Bündel (Maßnahmen, Dienste)

coax überreden

code Gesetzessammlung, Gesetzbuch, Signalsystem

co-determination Mitbestimmungsrechte

co-education Koedukation

coercion Zwang

coercive measures Zwangsmittel, Zwangsmaßnahme

coercive means Zwangsvollstreckung

cogent reasons zwingende Gründe

cognition Wahrnehmung, Erkenntnis

cohabitee Lebensgefährte

cohesion Zusammenhalt

cohort Altersgruppe (stat.)

commissioner Beauftragte/r

commitment Verpflichtung, Bindung (adm.) Einweisung

committee Ausschuss, Komitee

common law wife Lebensgefährtin

common law marriage eheähnliche Gemeinschaft

common weal Gemeinwohl

communal living Wohngemeinschaft

communal provision Gemeinschaftseinrichtung

community Gemeinschaft (auch Mitglieder einer Gemeinschaft)

community Gemeinschaft, Gemeinwesen, Gemeinde (auch i.S.v. Stadtgemeinde)

community action Gemeinwesenarbeit (politisiert)

community association Nachbarschaftsverein

community building Gemeinschaftsbildung, Gemeinschaftsförderung, Gemeindehaus (nicht notwendigerweise kirchlich)

community care gemeindenahe Betreuung (d.h. nicht in Heimen, Anstalten), Gemeindepflege (sen., psych.)

community development Gemeinwesenarbeit 🕮 social intervention

community home Erziehungsheim (früher approved school)

community medicine Sozialmedizin

community mental health centre ambulante bis teilstationäre, psychiatrisch-psychotherapeutische Versorgungsstelle

community nurse Gemeindeschwester

community planning Kommunalplanung

community psychiatry gemeindenahe Psychiatrie

community relations Verbesserung der Beziehungen in der Gemeinde, Gemeinschaftsbildung, Konfliktausgleich

community representative Gemeindesprecher, Gemeindevertreter (mit formalen Vertretungsrechten)

community service (UK) gemeinnützige Arbeit (anstelle von Freiheitsstrafe)

community service program (USA) Programm offener Hilfen (mit Bundesbeihilfen, Hauptquelle für die Arbeit freier Träger und Selbsthilfe-Gruppen)

community work Gemeinwesenarbeit 🕮 social intervention

compatibility Vereinbarkeit

compensation claim Ersatzanspruch (zwischen sozialen Leistungsträgern oder gegenüber verpflichteten anderen)

compensation Entschädigung, Ausgleich, Gehalt (USA)

compensatory education zusätzliche und/oder spezielle Unterrichtsangebote für benachteiligte Kinder

competence/competency Zuständigkeit, Befugnis, Fähigkeit

complain Beschwerde

complainant Beschwerdeführer/in

composure Haltung (inneres Gleichgewicht)

comprehensive agreements Gesamtvereinbarungen (Behindertenhilfe)

compulsion Zwang

compulsive symptom Zwangssymptom (psych.)

compulsory admission Zwangseinweisung

compulsory contribution Pflichtbeitrag (s.S.)

compulsory education allgemeine Schulpflicht

compulsory insurance Pflichtversicherung (s.S.)

compulsory measure Zwangsmaßnahme

compulsory zwingend, obligatorisch

concern Sache, Sorge, Belang

concession Abstrich (bei Forderungen)

conciliation Vermittlungsverfahren (z.B. Arbeitskampf, Ehekonflikt)

concomitant measure begleitende Maßnahme

condign punishment angemessene (schwere) Strafe

conduct disorder Verhaltensstörung (psych.)

conduct problem Führungsproblem, Verhaltensproblem

confidentiality Vertraulichkeit

confinement Beschränkung, Haft, Entbindung (med.)

conflict Konflikt

conflict avoidance Konfliktvermeidung

conflict management Konfliktbearbeitung

conflict resolution Konfliktlösung

congenital angeboren (z.B. Behinderung)

congregation Gemeinde (religiöse)

conjugal community (USA) eheliche Lebensgemeinschaft

conscientious objector Kriegsdienstverweigerer, Wehrdienstverweigerer

conscientisation Bewusstseinsbildung, Bewusstmachung (praktische Dimension des ⇒ awareness raising und der ⇒ politicisation)

conscious content Bewußtseinsinhalt

consciousness Bewusstsein

consciousness raising Bewusstseinsentwicklung

consciousness training Bewusstseinssteigerung

conscription Einberufung, Wehrpflicht

consecutive costs Folgekosten

consensus Konsens, Übereinstimung

constitution Verfassung, Satzung, Grundgesetz

constitutional law Verfassungsrecht

consultancy Beratungsstelle

consultant Berater/in, Gutachter/in

consultation Beratung, Einvernehmen

consultative processes Beratungsprozess, Abstimmungsprozess

consulting Beratung anbieten, Beratung

consumer advice Verbraucherberatung

contemporaries Gleichaltrige, Zeitgenossen

contestation Anfechtung

contestation of legitimacy Anfechtung der Ehelichkeit

continuous aid durchgehende Hilfe (durch Pflege)

continuous care ⇒ continuous aid

continuous support durchgehende Hilfe (Strafvollzug)

contraception Empfängnisverhütung

contract Vertrag

contract of employment Arbeitsvertrag

contradiction (in terms) Widerspruch (in sich selbst)

contribution Beitrag

contributory beitragspflichtig

control Kontrolle, Leitung (i.S.v. Aufsicht)

conviction Schuldspruch, Verurteilung, Überzeugung

co-operation Zusammenarbeit

co-operative (society) Genossenschaft

co-option Kooptierung

co-ordination Koordinierung, Abstimmung zwischen Trägern

co-ordinator Koordinator/in

co-payment Selbstbeteiligung

coping Lebensbewältigung (psych., soz.)

corporation Körperschaft

corporatist korporatistisch

correctional institution Erziehungsanstalt (jugendliche Straftäter)

correctiv measure Zuchtmittel (Jugendstrafrecht), Jugendstrafe (i.w.S., jun.)

corrective educational measure Erziehungsmaßregel

cost Kosten (auch: nichtmaterieller Art)

cost containment Kostenbegrenzung

cost retrenchment Kostendämpfung

costing Kostenberechnung (vorläufige)

council housing (UK) Sozialwohnungen (in öffentlichem Eigentum)

counselling Beratung (soz., päd., jun.), Berufsberatung

counsellor (interest) (USA) Berater/in (jur.)

countable anrechnungsfähig

counter culture Gegenkultur

court hearing Gerichtsverhandlung (Prozess)

court in full große Kammer (Gericht)

court order gerichtliche Verfügung

court session Gerichtsverhandlung

court decision Urteil, Entscheidung (gerichtlich)

crack synthetische Droge

creaming off lit.: Absahnen, verwendet als Heraussuchen "guter", d.h. lukrativer Fälle durch Trägerorganisationen

crèche Krippe

credit Kredit, anerkennen

criminal justice Strafgerichtsbarkeit, Strafrechtspflege

criminal law Strafrecht, Strafgesetz

criminal procedure Strafverfahren

criminal record Strafregister

criminal responsibility strafrechtliche Verantwortlichkeit, Zurechnungsfähigkeit

criminalise kriminalisieren

critical awareness kritisches Bewusstsein (vornehmlich rationaler Art)

critical consciousness kritisches Bewusstsein

critical mass kritische Größe

critique Kritik

cross community gemeindeübergreifend

crosscultural interkulturell

culpability (of an action) Schuldhaftigkeit, Sträflichkeit (einer Tat), Strafbarkeit

culture industry Kulturindustrie

culture jamming Veränderung des Inhalts von Werbeaussagen durch eine politisch oder kulturell alternative Aussage ⇒ adbusting

culture Kultur

curative heilend

curator (of an estate) (Nachlass-) Pflegschaft

curb zügeln

cure heilen

cure at a health resort Kur (Badekur) ⇒ spa

curfew Sperrstunde, (nächtliches) Ausgehverbot (für Kinder und Jugendliche) (USA)

curriculum vitae C.V. Lebenslauf

curtail kürzen, einschränken

custodial parent sorgeberechtigter Elternteil

custody Verwahrung, Sorgerecht der Eltern

cutback Kürzung (Mittel, Leistung), auch: draw back (wenn bestehende Leistungen zurückgenommen werden), selten short cut (wenn es um die Einführung von gering ausgestatteten Leistungssystemen geht)

– D –

daily allowance Tagegeld, Pflegesatz

data analysis Datenanalyse

data protection Datenschutz

daunt einschüchtern, entmutigen

day-care Tagespflege

day-care centre Tagespflegeheim, Kindertagesstätte

day hospital Tagesklinik

day nursery Kindergarten, Krippe

day treatment centre heilpädagogische/therapeutische Kindertagesstätte

deacon/ess Diakon, Diakonisse

dealer Rauschgifthändler

death grant einmalige Todesfallbeihilfe, Sterbegeld

debt Schuld (geschuldeter Betrag), Forderungen

decision Entscheidung

declaration of legal incompetence Entmündigung (jur.)

Declaration of legitimacy Ehelich(keits)erklärung

decline Abbau (med.)

decommodification Dekommodifikation, etwas "vom Markt nehmen", so anbieten, dass es nicht den Marktgesetzen der Preisregulierung unterliegt

decree Urteil, Erlass

decree nisi vorläufiges Scheidungsurteil

dedicated gewidmet, verpflichtet sein

dedication Hingabe

deductable abzugsfähig (Steuer)

default Verzug (jur.), auch Bestimmung

defence mechanism Abwehrmechanismus

defendant Angeklagte/r, Beklagte/r

deinstitutionalisation Herausnahme aus institutionalisierter Unterbringung (Heim, Anstalt)

delay Aufschub (z.B. Eingriff, Zahlung), Verzug (Fristüberschreitung)

demand Bedarf (Nachfrage)

demarcation Abgrenzung, Trennung, ⇒ distinction

dementia Demenz

democracy Demokratie

democratic demokratisch

demography Bevölkerungslehre

demonstrable aufzeigbar

demonstration Vorführung

denial of assistance unterlassene Hilfeleistung (jur.)

deny abstreiten

departmental supervision Dienstaufsicht

dependence Abhängigkeit

dependence allowance (USA) Kinderbeihilfe

dependence benefits (USA) Familienbeihilfe

deport abschieben

deportation Abschiebung (Ausländer)

deposition eidliche mündliche Zeugenaussage

depraved depraviert

depreciation Abwertung (psych.)

depressed deprimiert, verstimmt

depressive depressiv

deprivation Deprivation (psych., soz.)

deprivation of liberty Freiheitsentzug (jur.)

depth psychology Tiefenpsychologie

derelict baufällig

derive ableiten (auch im juristischen Sinn oder als Ableitung von Rechten)

descent Abstammung

deserving promotion förderungswürdig

design entwerfen, Entwurf

designation Bestimmung, Ernennung

destitution äußerste Armut, Verarmung

detachment process Ablösungsprozess (psych.)

detain festhalten, in Haft halten

detention centre (UK) Jugendstrafanstalt

detention Festnahme, Haft

deterioration Verschlechterung

determination Bestimmung, starker Wille, fester Wille

detoxi(fi)cation Entgiftung (von einem Suchtmittel)

developer Entwickler/in

development Entwicklung

development plan Erschließungsplan (Flächennutzungsplan)

developmental disorder Entwicklungsstörung (med., psych.)

deviance Abweichung (soziologisch, sozial, statistisches Maß)

deviant behaviour abweichendes Verhalten, Verhaltensauffälligkeit

deviate abweichen

dialogue Dialog

different unterschiedlich

dignity of man Menschenwürde

direct action direkte Aktion zur Verhinderung eines Ereignissses oder der Veränderung von Bestehendem, (oft) mit körperlichem Einsatz

direct provision Ausgabe von Wohlfahrtsleistungen als "Naturalleistung" (einschließlich Gutscheinen etc.)

direction Auflage, Weisung, allgemein: Richtung

directive Direktive, Anweisung, pedantische Ausführung

directory Verzeichnis

directory provisions Sollvorschrift (jur.)

disability Behinderung, Arbeitsunfähigkeit

disable behindern

disadvantage Benachteiligung

disaster Katastrophe

discharge Entlassung (Gefängnis, Armee, aber insbesondere Krankenhaus [⇒ release]), Entlastung (Schuld), freisprechen

discharged psychiatric patient aus der Psychiatrie entlassener Patient

disclose offenbaren

discourse Diskurs

discretionary decision Ermessensentscheidung

discretion Ermessen

discursive diskursiv

discussion Diskussion

disencumbrance Entschuldung

disengage Abstand nehmen, Verbindung auflösen

disgression Vertraulichkeit

disparagement Verunglimpfung, Abwertung

dispensable entbehrlich

dispensary (früherer Begriff, kaum noch verwendet) Apotheke ⇒ pharmacy, chemist's

dispense verteilen (Medikamente, Spenden), erlassen (Verpflichtung, Kosten)

displace verdrängen, verschleppen (Personen)

disposition Veranlagung, Neigung

disregarded assets Schonvermögen (soz.)

dissocial (USA) asozial (abwertend)

dissonance Unstimmigkeit

dissonant unstimmig

distinction Abgrenzung, Unterscheidung ⇒ demarcation

distrain upon sb. pfänden (Person)

distraint Zwangsvollsstreckung

distress Hilfebedürftigkeit, akute Notsituation

distressed area Notstandsgebiet

distributing authority bereitstellende Verwaltung

diverse vielfältig

diversion Herausnahme (aus dem Jugendstrafvollzug), Ablösung von Strafe durch Erziehungsmaßnahme

diversity Vielfalt

divorce Scheidung

DIY-culture Heimwerkermentalität

document Urkunde, Beleg

documentary Tatsachenbericht

domestic häuslich

domestic violence häusliche Gewalt (Gebrauch eher mit allgemeinem Bezug zu gewaltsamen Verhältnissen, Gebrauch vor allem auch im politischen Bereich und Sinn von ⇒ batter

domicile fester Aufenthaltsort, Wohnsitz

domiciled ansässig

domiciliary care Betreuung in der Wohnung

donation Spende, Schenkung, Stiftung

donor Spender (med., soz.)

dope Rauschmittel

dossier Akte**dormitory** Schlafsaal, Schlafstatt

down-payment Anzahlung (Ratenkauf)

drink Getränk (auch als Suchtmittel)

drop-in-centre Treff

drop-out Aussteiger

drug Droge, Arznei

drug abuse Drogenmissbrauch

drug addiction Drogensucht

drug control Drogenbekämpfung

drug counselling Drogenberatung

drug dependency Drogenabhängigkeit

drug taker Drogenkonsument

drug taking Drogenkonsum

drug therapy Drogentherapie

drug trafficking Drogenhandel

drug treatment Drogenentwöhnung, Drogenentzug

drug use Drogenkonsum

drug withdrawal Drogenentzug

due fällig, zustehend, vorschriftsmäßig

due process of law ordnungsgemäßes Ermessen

duty to work Arbeitspflicht

duty of supervision (parental) Aufsichtspflicht (Eltern)

dyslexia Legasthenie, Lese-Rechtschreib-Schwäche

– E –

early detection Früherkennung (med.)

early retirement vorzeitige Pensionierung

early childhood development frühkindliche

earmark hervorheben, widmen, ausrichten auf (to earmark an amount)

earn a living Lebensunterhalt verdienen (auch: make a living out of something)

earnings test, more frequently: means test Einkommensprüfung

earnings-disregard Einkommens-Freibetrag

economic development wirtschaftliche Entwicklung

economic efficiency Wirtschaftlichkeit (Haushaltsführung, Hilfeleistung)

economically vulnerable einkommensschwach

economistic ökonomistisch

editor Herausgeber (auch im Sinne eines "erweiterten Korrekturlesens")

education Erziehung, Bildung

education grant öffentliches Stipendium

education(al)ist Erziehungswissenschaftler/in, Pädagoge/in

educational leave Bildungsurlaub

educational measures Erziehungsmaßnahmen

educational-assistance Erziehungsbeihilfe

educator Erzieher/in

effectivity analysis Nutzwertanalyse

efficiency Effizienz

electronic data processing elektronische Datenverarbeitung

eligibility Wählbarkeit, Eignung, Anspruchsberechtigung, Anwartschaft

eligible wählbar, geeignet, anspruchsberechtigt

embargo Embargo

embarrassment Verlegenheit (auch: Geldverlegenheit)

emergence Auftauchen, Entstehung

emergency admission Notaufnahme

emergency alarm Notrufanlage

emergency Notstand, Notfall

emergency payment (UK) Vorauszahlung auf strittige oder verzögerte Pflichtleistungen anderer Träger durch das Sozialamt

emergency relief Nothilfe

emergency service Notdienst

emergency shelter Notunterkunft, Auffangheim (z.B. für jugendliche Wegläufer) (soz., jur.).

emotionally disturbed emotional (psychisch) gestört

empathy Betroffenheit (i.S.v. Einfühlung)

empirical social research empirische Sozialforschung

employ beschäftigen

employability Beschäftigungsfähigkeit

employer Arbeitgeber/in

Employment and training programmes Beschäftigungs- und Ausbildungsprogramme

Employment office (USA) Arbeitsamt

Employment services (UK) behördliche Arbeitsvermittlung und Rehabilitation

employment agency Stellenvermittlung

empowerment 📖 Empowerment

enablement Befähigung (der Klienten durch Sozialarbeiter) 📖 empowerment

enabling befähigen 📖 empowerment

encounter Begegnung, Auseinandersetzung

enculturation Enkulturation (soziol.)

endemic örtlich begrenzt

Endogenous von innen kommend, endogen

endorsement Bestätigung, Genehmigung, Klausel

Endowment assurance (UK) **endowment insurance** (USA) Lebensversicherung (Kapitalversicherung auf den Erlebensfall)

endowment Stiftung (Schenkung)

enforced payment Zwangsgeld (jur.)

enforcement Erzwingung, Vollstreckung

enforcement by law Zwangsmittel (jur.)

enforcement by writ Zwangsvollstreckung (jur.)

engagement Einstellung (Arbeitskräfte), Verpflichtung, Verlöbnis

enhancement Bewusstseinserweiterung (psych.)

enjoin auferlegen, vorschreiben

enlistement (USA) Militärdienst

enterprise allowance scheme (UK) staatlicher Zuschuss zur Unternehmensgründung

entitlement Befugnis, Berechtigung (jur.) of residence Aufenthaltsberechtigung

entity Einheit

entrant (USA) Ausländer, Zuwanderer (mit ungeklärtem Rechtsstatus)

enuresis Bettnässen

environment Milieu, Umgebung (soziol.), Umfeld (psych., soziol.)

envisage gedenken etwas zu tun, ins Auge fassen, sich etwas vorstellen

epidemic Seuche

equal treatment Gleichbehandlung (von Männern und Frauen)

equality Gleichheit – allgemein verwendet, auch politisch und sozial

equality of rights Gleichberechtigung

equity Gerechtigkeit, Gleichheit vor allem mit ökonomischem Bezug, d.h. hinsichtlich der "ökonomischen Macht"

escape fliehen, entkommen

escapism Realitätsflucht (psych.)

escort service Begleitdienst (soziol.)

established post Planstelle

establishment Anstalt

estate agency (USA) Wohnungsvermittlung

estate management Nachlassverwaltung, Wohnsiedlungsverwaltung, oftmals partizipativ ausgerichtet

estate Nachlass, Erbmasse, Grundstück

estimate Voranschlag (adm.)

ethnic minority ethnische Minderheit

evacuee Evakuierte/r, Aussiedler/in

evening classes Abendschule, Fortbildungskurs

evening school Abendschule, Fortbildungskurs

eviction Zwangsräumung

eviction notice (UK) Räumungsbefehl (jur.)

evidence Beweis, Zeugnis

ex officio von Amts wegen

exchange Austausch

exchange value Tauschwert

execution Durchführung, Pfändung, Vollstreckung

execution sale (USA) Zwangsversteigerung

executive Verwaltung (Staatsgewalt im Sinne der Gewaltenteilung), ausführendes Organ

exemption Befreiung (Steuern)

exhibition Ausstellung

exigency Notlage, Dringlichkeit

exogeneous durch äußere Umstände bedingt

expedient zweckdienlich

expel austreiben, verweisen, ausweisen

expenditure Aufwand, Auslage, Ausgabe

expert Experte

expert status Expertenstatus

expertise Gutachten, Sachkenntnis

expiration Ablauf, Erlöschen

exploration Untersuchung

expulsion Ausweisung

extended family Großfamilie

extension Erweiterung, Telefondurchwahl

extramarital außerehelich (Beziehung)

extra-pay (Gehalts-)Zulage

extra-curricular education außerschulische Bildung

– F –

facilitate erleichtern, ermöglichen

facilitation Moderation

facilitator Moderator/in

facility Einrichtung

factual tatsächlich

factual situation Tatbestand

failure Misserfolg, Versäumnis

familiarisation Eingewöhnung (Arbeitsplatz, Umgebung)

family Familie

family advice centre (UK) Familienberatungsstelle

family allowance Familienbeihilfe, Familienzuschlag

family counselling Familienberatung

family court Familiengericht, Jugendgericht (USA)

family credit (UK) Familienfreibetra,g Familienunterstützung (soz.)

family income supplement (UK) Verdienst für Personen mit mindestens einem abhängigen Kind

family law Familienrecht

family maintenance Familienunterhalt

family member Familienangehörige/r

family placement Familienunterbringung (jun.)

family policy Familienpolitik

family rate (USA) Familienermäßigung (Bahnfahrten, Eintritt usw.)

family reconciliation Familienzusammenführung (eher nach Konflikt, s.a. ⇒ family reunion)

family reunion Familienzusammenführung (eher nach "künstlicher" Trennung, s.a. ⇒ family reconciliation)

family therapy Familientherapie

family ties Familienbindung

family welfare Familienhilfe

father ein Kind zeugen, Vater

feasibility Durchführbarkeit

feasibility study Machbarkeitsstudie

feature Charakteristikum

feminist Frauenrechtler/in, Feminist/in

field-research Feldforschung

field office Außenstelle

field work Feldarbeit

field worker Außendienstarbeiter, insbesondere im Sozialbereich, auch bei empirischen Erhebungen

file Akte

file keeping Aktenführung

foreigner Ausländer/in
📖 Ausländer

formal formal, förmlich (auch hinsichtlich des Auftretens, Erscheinens)

fortress Festung, Abschottung

foster parents Pflegeeltern

friendly freundlich

friendship Freundschaft

future search conference "Visions- und Planungskonferenz" einer Gemeinde/Gemeinschaft

– G –

gaming spielerische Art der Informationsgewinnung, gezielter Einsatz von Spielen

gated Einschließung

gay homosexuell

gender Geschlecht (als soziales Konstrukt)

general allgemein

generation Generation, Generierung

generative themes Wesensbegriffe, Bestimmung wesentlicher Faktoren in einem Gemeinwesen *(Verwendung bei Paolo Freire)*

gipsies Sinti, Roma, Zigeuner 🕮 traveller

gloss over vertuschen, beschönigen

governance Regierungsgefüge. Gemeint ist dieses in seiner Gesamtheit als komplexes und prozesshaftes Gefüge (einschließlich semi- und informaler Strukturen und Beteiligungsverhältnisse, bis zu einem gewissen Grad auch politische Kultur umfassend)

government Regierung

grant Zuschuss, Beihilfe, gewähren, bewilligen, zugeben

guarantee Garantie, bürgen

guardian ad litem (UK) Jugendgerichtshelfer/in

guardian Vormund

guardianship court Vormundschaftsgericht

guardianship Vormundschaft, Pflegschaft

guidance counsellor Psychologe zur Beratung Jugendlicher

guidance Führung, Leitung, Richtlinie

guide dog (UK) Blindenhund

gypsies ⇒ gipsies 🕮 traveller

– H –

habitable bewohnbar

habituee Eingeweihter, Ortskundiger, Sachkundiger

handicap Behinderung

handicapped behindert, Behinderte/r

handling Behandlung (eines Vorganges)

happening Ereignis, (Kunst) Happening

hard labour (USA) Zwangsarbeit

hardship Not, Elend

hate Hass, hassen

hate-crime Kriminalität aus Gründen des Hasses des angenommenen Status des Opfers (z.B. Rassismus)

haves and have-nots Besitzende und Besitzlose

hazard Gefahr, Risiko, riskieren, zu sagen wagen

head start program (USA) Bundesprogramm für bildungsbenachteiligte Kinder

heal (a breach) (v.) heilen (Zerwürfnis)

health cure Heilkur

health department Gesundheitsamt

health education Gesundheitserziehung, Gesundheitsaufklärung

health fund Krankenkasse

health insurance Krankenversicherung

health maintenance organisation (HMO) (USA) gemeinnützige Krankenversicherungsvereine mit fallweiser Selbstbeteiligung

health office Gesundheitsamt

health work Gesundheitsfürsorge

health worker Gesundheitsfürsorger

health-center Poliklinik

hearing Anhörung, (Gerichts-)Verhandlung

hearing defect Hörbehinderung

hegemony Hegemonie, Vorherrschaft

heir Erbe, Nachlass

helper-syndrome Helfersyndrom

helpline ⇒ hotline

hereditary trait Anlage (biol.)

hereditary-disease Erbkrankheit

higher authority vorgesetzte Behörde

parade auch: politischer Umzug

hire-purchase contract Abzahlungsvertrag

home control Heimaufsicht (jun.,sen.)

holistic development ganzheitliche Entwicklung, ganzheitliche Orientierung

holistic ganzheitlich

home delivered meals (USA) Essen auf Rädern

home for the elderly Alten(pflege)heim

home help Hauspfleger/in (D: jetzt Familienpfleger/In)

home help service Hauspflegedienst (Kindererziehung, Krankenpflege, Haushalt)

home manager Heimleiter/in

home-care häusliche Pflege

homeless obdachlos, Obdachlose, Nichtsesshaftigkeit 🕮 Nomadentum

homemaker (USA) Hauspfleger/in

Homemaker service (USA) Hauspflegedienst

homosexual homosexuell

honorary office Ehrenamt

hospice Sterbeklinik

hospice care Hospizpflege (Sterbepflege)

hospital allowance Krankenhauspflegesatz

hospital Krankenhaus, psychiatrische Klinik (USA)

hospital social work Sozialarbeit im Krankenhaus

hostel Heim, Herberge, Obdachlosenunterkunft

hostile attitude feindselige Haltung

hotline Notruf (Telefon, Sprechanlage)

house for battered women Frauenhaus, more frequently: women's refuge

household effects Hausrat

houses in multiple occupation (HMO) (UK) Miethäuser, Hotels (Gegensatz zu Eigenheim)

housing advice centre (UK) Wohnungsberatung

housing allowance Mietbeihilfe

housing assistance (USA) soziale Hilfen für Mieter oder Eigentümer

housing association Wohnungs(bau)genossenschaft, Wohnungsverein

housing benefit "Wohngeld", Wohnkostenzuschuss, Wohnkostenerstattung

housing crisis Wohnungs(markt)krise

housing department (UK) Wohnungsamt

housing Wohnungswesen, Unterkunft

human dignity Menschenwürde

human rights Menschenrechte

humanitarian relief humanitäre Hilfe

humanity Menschlichkeit, Menschheit

hunger Hunger (for knowledge: nach Wissen, Wissensdurst)

– I –

institutional racism Rassismus in einer und durch eine Institution, ein Amt, eine Einrichtung

ideas Ideen

identity Identität

identity card Personalausweis

illegal rechtswidrig

illegitimacy Gesetzwidrigkeit, Nichtehelichkeit

illegitimate gesetzeswidrig, nicht ehelich (Kind)

illicit trade Schwarzhandel

illiteracy Analphabetentum

illiterate ungebildet

immaturity Mangel an Reife

immigrant Einwanderer

immigrant labourers (workers) ausländische Arbeiter

immigration Einwanderung

immiseration absolute Verelendung

impaired sensory function Sinnesbehinderung

impairment Behinderung, Schädigung (vor allem im Zusammenhang mit visual impairment als Sehbehinderung, hearing impairment Hörbehinderung)

impartial unparteiisch, objektiv

impartiality Objektivität (Unparteilichkeit)

impede jemanden/etwas behindern

implementation Ausführung

implication Folge, Andeutung, Folgerung

impound sicherstellen

impoverishment Verarmung (Vorgang)

impractical unpraktisch, undurchführbar

imprecise ungenau

inability to practice one's profession Berufsunfähigkeit

incapacitated arbeits-, erwerbsunfähig, körperlich (geistig) behindert

incarceration Einsperrung

inclusion Einschließung, Einbeziehung

inclusive einschließen

inclusivity einbeziehende Offenheit

incomplete unvollständig

incompetent unfähig, unzuständig, unzurechnungsfähig (USA)

incontinence Unmäßigkeit, Inkontinenz (med.)

incorporated eingetragen (US-Vereinsrecht)

incorporation Vereinigung, Zusammenschluss, Eingliederung, Eintragung

increase Zunahme, Verstärkung, Wachstum

incrementalism Stückwerk

incriminating belastend (jur.)

incurred auf sich laden (von Schulden, Strafe etc.)

incursion Eindringen, feindlicher Einfall

indebtedness Verschuldung

indemnity Entschädigung (jur.), Absicherung, Immunität

indeterminate unbestimmt, ungewiss

indication Indikation (med., psych.)

indict anklagen

indifferent gleichgültig, unerheblich

indigenous einheimisch, angeboren

indiscriminate kritiklos, wahllos, ungeordnet

individual individuell, einzeln (e.g. auch **individual case** einzelner Fall)

individuality Individualität (Persönlichkeit)

industrial industriell

industrialised industriell entwickelt

industry Industrie

ineffective unwirksam, wirkungslos

infant care Säuglingspflege

infant Minderjährige/r, Kind, Säugling

infant mortality Säuglingssterblichkeit

infant welfare Säuglingsfürsorge

infirmity Gebrechen

informal informell, formlos

informal support network informelles Netz persönlicher Hilfen

informal economy Schattenwirtschaft

informative informativ

infrastructure Infrastruktur

in-group eigene Gruppe (soziol.)

in-group home child care Kinderbetreuung zu Hause

in-group home nursing (USA) häusliche Pflege

in-group patient stationär (med.)

in-group service-training (USA) betriebliche Ausbildung, berufsbegleitende Fortbildung

inhalants Schnüffeldrogen

inheritance Erbschaft, auch geistige Erbschaft

inhibition Hemmung

initiate initiieren

initiative Initiative

Innate angeboren

innovate erneuern

innovation Erneuerung

innovative auf Erneuerungen zielend, Erneuerungen anstrebend und verwirklichend

inquiry Nachforschung, Anhörung

insanitary gesundheitsschädlich

insanity (veraltet) Geisteskrankheit

inspection Untersuchung

inspectorate (UK) Aufsichtsbehörde

institute einrichten, einleiten, (in ein Amt) einsetzen, Institut, Einrichtung

institution (feststehende) Einrichtung, Anstalt, Einführung

institutional upbringing Heimerziehung (jun.)

institutional care Anstaltspflege

institutionalisation Unterbringung in einer Einrichtung

instruction Dienstanweisung, Handlungsanleitung

instructor Anleiter/in

instrument Instrument

instrumental instrumentell

insulation (USA) Vereinsamung

insurance Versicherung

integral wesentlich

integration Eingliederung (Behinderte, Ausländer, Umsiedler)

integrity Integrität

interaction Interaktion

interconnection Verbund

interdisciplinary interdisziplinär

interest Interesse, Zins

intergovernmental internationale Zusammenarbeit zwischen Regierungen/Gremien, ohne (a) die Selbstständigkeit der Beteiligten aufzuheben und (b) eine eigenständige, zusätzliche Einheit darzustellen 🕮 international

intermediary intermediär

intermediate zwischen ...

internal migration Binnenwanderung

internalisation Internalisierung

international 🕮 international

internationalism Internationalismus 🕮 international

interpretation Interpretation, sinngemäße Übersetzung

interpretative interpretierend (vor allem in der Bezeichnung interpretative Soziologie)

interpreter Übersetzer/in

interrogation Verhör

intimidation Einschüchterung

invalid ungültig, rechtsunwirksam

invalidity Dienstunfähigkeit

investigation Untersuchung

invoke erflehen

involuntary unfreiwillig (allgemein, nicht so sehr "gezwungen")

involve einbeziehen

isolation Vereinsamung

issue (v.) erlassen (Bestimmung, Gesetz), Erlass, Streitfrage, Thema

issue-based interessengeleitet

issue-based idenity building interessengeleitete Indentitätsbildung

– J –

jamming hineinpressen

janitor Pförtner, (USA) Hausmeister

jargon Redeweise

job centre (UK) staatliche Arbeitsvermittlung

job division (USA) ⇒ job sharing

Job Opportunities in the Business Sectors (JOBS) (USA) Ausbildung und Beschäftigung für schwer Vermittelbare in der Privatwirtschaft mit Hilfe eines Bundesprogramms

job preservation Arbeitsplatzerhaltung

job protection Arbeitsplatzschutz

job release (UK) vorzeitiger Ruhestand (Bedingung, dass Jüngere nachrücken)

job security Sicherheit des Arbeitsplatzes

job seeker Arbeitsuchende/r

job sharing Aufteilung eines Vollzeitarbeitsplatzes auf zwei oder mehrere Personen

jobs club Arbeitslosentreff

joint vocational training überbetriebliche Ausbildung

judgement Urteil

judicator Rechtsprechung (Justiz)

judicial officer Rechtspfleger/in

judiciary Rechtspflege

junk food minderwertiges Massenessen

junkie Fixer/in

jurisdiction Gerichtsbarkeit (jur.), Rechtsprechung (Gerichtsurteil)

juror Geschworene/r, Preisrichter/in

jury Geschworene, Schöffen, Sachverständigenausschuss

justice Gerechtigkeit (to, gegen)

juvenile court Jugendgericht

juvenile delinquency Jugendkriminalität, (USA: häufig nur Verstöße gegen Jugendschutzrecht [status offenses] einschließlich Schulpflicht, Ausgangsbeschränkungen [curfew] usw.)

juvenile jugendlich (jur., med.)

juvenile justice Jugendgerichtsbarkeit

juvenile prosecutor Jugendstaatsanwalt, Jugendstaatsanwältin

– K –

key worker Schlüsselperson (Leistung von direkter, individueller Unterstützung)

kindergarten Kindertagesstätte mit Vorschulprogramm, (USA: Vorschule für 5- bis 7-jährige

kinesitherapy Bewegungstherapie

kinship Sippenverband, erweiterte Familie (soziol.) ⇒ sibling (Geschwister) ⇒ relative (Verwandter), ähnlich kinship

– L –

label Vorurteil, Etikettierung, Einordnung

labelling approach Etikettierungsansatz (soziol.)

labour contract (USA) kollektiver Arbeitsvertrag

labour administration Arbeitsverwaltung

labour court Arbeitsgericht

labour exchange Arbeitsvermittlung

labour office Arbeitsamt

labour reserve Arbeitskraftreserve

labourer ungelernte/r Arbeiter/in

laid-off entlassen

lay therapist (USA) Laie, der sich ständig intensiv um Problemfälle (Familien) kümmert

laissez faire gewähren lassen (im wirtschaftsliberalistischen Sinn, auch bei der Kindererziehung)

law guardian (USA) Jugenderichtshelfer/in

law of inheritance Erbrecht (jur.)

law Recht, Rechtsgebiet

lawful legitim, legal

lay down conditions (v.) Bedingungen festsetzen

lay-off (v.) entlassen (Personal)

layette Säuglingsausstattung

lead Führung, Leitung, auch: führende Stelle, Vorsprung

leader Leiter/in

leadership Leitung

learner Lernende/r

learning disability Lernstörung (psych.)

learning disablement neurotische Lernstörung (nicht Lernbehinderung)

learning target Lernziel (päd.)

leave Urlaub

legal advice centre (UK) Rechtsberatungsstelle (soz.)

legal aid and advice (UK) Rechtshilfe (soz.)

legal aid bureau (USA) Rechtsberatungstelle (soz.)

legal capability Zurechnungsfähigkeit (jur.)

legal capacity Rechtsfähigkeit

legal claim Rechtsanspruch

legal counsel Beistand (jur.)

legal counselling Rechtsberatung

legal hearing rechtliches Gehör

legal instruction Rechtsmittelbelehrung

legal redress Rechtsmittel

legal remedy Rechtsbehelf

legal representative gesetzliche/r Vertreter/in

legally binding rechtskräftig

legally competent geschäftsfähig (jur.)

legislate Gesetz erlassen

legislation Gesetzgebung

legislative gesetzgebend

legislature gesetzgebende Körperschaft

legitimate legitim

leisure society Freizeitgesellschaft

leisure time guidance Freizeitbetreuung

lesbian lesbisch, Lesbierin, Lesbe

less gifted minderbegabt

liability Haftung

liable for a fee gebührenpflichtig

liberal großzügig, freigebig, freigeistig

liberation Befreiung (auch ideologisch, e.g. liberations theology Befreiungstheologie)

library Bücherei, Bibliothek

life assurance Lebensversicherung

link in networking sich (an ein Netzwerk) anschließen

link-up organisatorische Verknüpfung, Aneinanderreihen

literacy campaign Alphabetisierungskampagne

livliehood Lebensunterhalt

loan Darlehen

loan shark Kredithai

local action örtliche Initiative

local administration Verwaltung auf örtlicher Ebene

local agency örtlicher Träger

local authority Gemeinde (Verwaltungsstellen)

local politics Gemeindepolitik

local social services department (UK) Sozialamt

locality Örtlichkeit, Ort, Stelle

lodge an appeal (v.) Einspruch einlegen

logical logisch, folgerichtig

loiterer Herumtreiber/in (Streuner/in)

long term care allowance Pflegegeld

lot Bürde, Schicksal, Los

lottery funding durch Lotterieeinnahmen gefördert

lottery ticket Los

– M –

machine Maschine

magistrate Laienrichter/in

mainstream Hauptrichtung, hauptsächlich

mainstreaming
🕮 mainstreaming

maintenance Versorgung (für Beamte, Miltärangehörige, Kriegsopfer), Unterhalt

maintenance assistance Unterhaltshilfe

maintenance office Versorgungsamt (Kriegsopfer)

maintenance responsibility Unterhaltspflicht (allg.)

major groß, bedeutend, wichtig, volljährig

majority Mündigkeit, mündig, Mehrheit

maladjusted verhaltensgestört, unangepasst

maladministration schlechte, fehlerhafte Verwaltung

malfeasance Gesetzesübertretung (jur.), Amtsmissbrauch (jur.)

malpractice Verstoß (gegen Berufs- und Standesethos), Fehlverhalten

manage beherrschen (schaffen), zu Stande bringen, handhaben

Management Leitung (Betrieb)

management of public affairs (USA) Verwaltungsapparat

manager Verwalter/in, Führungskraft, Geschäftsführer/in

mandatory provision zwingende Vorschrift (jur.)

manual alphabet (in sign language) Fingersprache, Gebärdensprache (Taubstumme), Zeichensprache 🕮 sign language

map Karte, Plan, ein Gebiet erfassen, kartographieren

mapping inhaltlich abgrenzen, bestimmen

marginal unbedeutend, gering

marginalise ausgrenzen, an den Rand drängen

marginalised group Randgruppe

marital breakdown Ehescheitern

marital status Familenstand

market basket Warenkorb (stat.)

market Markt

marketing Werbung, Herausstellen

marriage counselling Eheberatung (soz.)

martyr Märtyrer(in)

mass media Massenmedien

mass meeting Großkundgebung

mass mobilisation Mobilisierung einer Menge von Menschen, “etwas bewegen“, “jemanden bewegen“, motivieren

mass society Massengesellschaft

masterplan Grund(lagen)orientierung

maternity allowance (UK) Mutterschaftsgeld

maternity benefit (UK) Mutterschaftsgeld (für Berufstätige)

maternity grant (UK) Entbindungspauschale (soz.)

maternity leave Mutterschaftsurlaub

maternity pay (UK) Gehaltsfortzahlung bei Mutterschaft

maternity protection Mutterschutz (einschließlich Kündigungsschutz)

matrix Matrix, Keimschicht

matron Heimleiterin

meagre dürftig

meals on wheels Essen auf Rädern

meals on wheels services Mahlzeitendienste

means test (UK) Bedürftigkeitsprüfung (soz.)

means-tested entitlement Anspruch aufgrund einer Bedürftigkeitsprüfung (Sozialhilfe) (soz.)

mechanical mechanisch

media Medien

mediating Weitervermittlung (von Klienten an geeignete Hilfsquellen) (soz., jun.), vermitteln (auch zwischen Konfliktparteien)

mediation Vermittlung (Streitigkeit)

mediator Vermittler/in

medicaid (USA) Sozialhilfeleistung bei Krankheit und Mutterschaft

medical care Versorgung (med.)

medical model Erklärung von sozialen Umständen, Verhaltensweisen etc. durch (vorgebliche) medizinische Faktoren und Bedingungen, verbunden mit einer expertokratischen Herangehensweise

medical referee (USA) Amtsarzt, Amtsärztin

medical officer Amtsarzt, Amtsärztin

medicare (USA) Kranken- und Pflegeversicherung der Rentner

mediocre mittelmäßig

meeting point Treffpunkt (jun., sen.)

meeting Treffen (sowohl offiziell als auch informell und/oder zufällig)

menial untergeordnet, niedrig (Arbeit)

mental disorder Geistesstörung (med., psych.)

mental health geistige Gesundheit

mental hospital psychiatrisches Krankenhaus

mental hygiene (WHO) geistige Hygiene (im Deutschen stark ideologisch besetzt)

mental illness psychische Krankheit, geistige Behinderung

mentally disabled geistig behindert, geistig Behinderte(r)

meritocracy Leistungsgesellschaft

meritocratic auf die Leistungsgesellschaft bezogen, deren Grundsätze verwirklichend

meshing Vernetzung (nicht sehr geläufiger Begriff)

mess Unordnung, Durcheinander

method Methode

methodology Methodologie

midwife Hebamme (med.)

migrant worker Wanderarbeiter/in, ausländische/r Arbeiter/in

migration Bevölkerungsbewegung, Migration

mild retardation Lernbehinderung (psych.)

mind aufpassen

mind-setting einstimmen

mine workers pension, mine workers health insurance knappschaftliche Renten-, Krankenversicherung

minimum of subsistence Existenzminimum

minimum standards Mindeststandard

minister Seelsorger/in, diplomatische/r Geschäftsträger/in, Minister/in

minor minderjährig, Minderjährige/r

minority Unmündigkeit, Minderheit (soziale Gruppe) (soziol.)

misdemeanour Vergehen, Ordnungswidrigkeit (jur.)

misery Elend, Not (soz.)

mitigation of sentence Strafmilderung

mix Mischung, vermengen

mixed gemischt

mobile library Fahrbücherei

mobilisation Mobilisierung, Aktivierung

mobilise mobilisieren, aktivieren

mobility allowance (UK) Mobilitätsbeihilfe (Zuschuss für Behinderte zur Fortbewegung und erleichterten Teilnahme am gesellschaftlichen Leben, auch Freifahrt u.ä)

mock-up Attrappe

model action beispielgebende Aktion

modelling modellieren

moderator Moderator/in

modicum geringes, bescheidenes Ausmaß

molestation Belästigung (insbes. von Frauen, Kindern)

monitoring begleitende Studie

morbid krankhaft (Zustand)

mortality Sterblichkeit

mortgage Hypothek, Pfandverschreibung

mother bemuttern, Mutter

mother and infant clinic Mütterberatungsstelle (med.)

motor Motor, fahren

motorised motorisiert

movement Bewegung (soziol.)

multiple deprivation Benachteiligung in mehrfacher Hinsicht

multiple vielfach

municipal authorities (USA) städtische Verwaltung

municipality Gemeinde (Verwaltungsbezirk)

mutual gegenseitig, 📖 solidarity

mutual adaptation Angleichung (Gesetze, Maßnahmen)

mutual insurance fund Genossenschaftskasse (Versicherung)

mutual judical assistance Rechtshilfe (unter Gerichten) (jur.)

mutual savings bank Genossenschaftssparkasse

– N –

name Name

Narcotics Act (USA) Betäubungsmittelgesetz

narcotics Betäubungsmittel (med.), Drogen aller Art (USA)

nation state Nationalstaat

national national

national service Wehrdienst

nationality Staatsangehörigkeit (jur.) ⇒ 🕮 citizenship

native gebürtig

natural natürlich

natural helpers natürliche Helfer

naturalisation Einbürgerung 🕮 citizenship

nature Natur

nature and nurture Anlage und Umwelt

necessary notwendig

necessity Notwendigkeit

need Bedürfnis, Bedarf

neediness Bedürftigkeit

needs basket Warenkorb (soz.)

negation Verneinung, Aufhebung

neglect Verwahrlosung (Kinder)

negligible amount Bagatellbetrag

neighbourhood aid Nachbarschaftshilfe

neighbourhood health centre (USA) kostenfreie Versorgung für Unversicherte und Notfälle mit ärztlichen und verwandten Leistungen

neighbourhood Nachbarschaft

neighbourhood watch Programm der Wachsamkeit in der Nachbarschaft

network Netzwerk

networking Vernetzung

newsletter Rundbrief

newspaper Zeitung

night care Übernachtung und Versorgung für Hilfebedürftige

night clinic teilstationäre psychiatrische Versorgung mit Übernachtung (psych.), Spätsprechstunde in Polyklinik (med.)

night college Abendgymnasium

night watch Nachtwache, nächtlicher Sicherheitsdienst

no abnormality discernible (n.a.d.) ohne Befund (psych.)

no appreciable disease (n.a.d.) ohne Befund (med.)

no go area Sperrgebiet, Sperrzone

non-stop ununterbrochen

non-contributory beitragsfrei

non-family household Wohngemeinschaft

non-governmental organisations freie Verbände
📖 Wohlfahrtsverband

non-probational offenses (USA) Verbrechen, bei denen laut Gesetz Bewährung, Strafaussetzung oder vorzeitige Entlassung ausgeschlossen ist (jur.)

non-profit organisation gemeinnützige Organisation
📖 Wohlfahrtsverband

non-recurring supplements einmalige Beihilfen (in Verbindung mit laufenden Zahlungen)

nonsense Unsinn

non-statutory nichtstaatlich, privat, freiwillig

notable beachtenswert

note-taking Aufzeichnen, Mitschreiben

noteworthy bemerkenswert

notice of approval Genehmigungsbescheid

notice of ejectment (USA) Räumungsbefehl

notice of rejection Ablehnungsbescheid

notice of termination Kündigung aussprechen

notification Benachrichtigung

notify benachrichtigen

nuclear arsenal Atomwaffenfabrik, Atomwaffenlager

nuclear family Kleinfamilie, Kernfamilie

nuclear power Atommacht

nuclear weaponry Atombewaffnung

null and void null und nichtig

nullified aufheben, für nichtig erklären

nurse Kinderpflegerin, Krankenschwester, Pflegerin

nursery Tagesheim

nursery aid Kindergartenhelfer/in

nursery education Kindergartenerziehung

nursery educator Kindergartenerzieher/in (mit Erzieherausbildung)

nursery nurse Kindergartenschwester

nursery school Vorschule für 3-bis 4-jährige Kinder

nursery teacher Kindergartenpädagoge, Kindergartenpädagogin (päd.)

nursing allowance Pflegezulage (Kriegsblinde und andere Schwerkriegsbeschädigte)

nursing benefit Pflegegeld (bei häuslicher Pflege)

nursing contract Pflegevertrag

nursing home Pflegeheim

nursing ward Pflegeabteilung

nurture Erziehung, Umwelteinfluss, emotionale Förderung

– O –

objection Einspruch (adm., jur.)

objectivity Objektivität (Sachlichkeit)

obligation Bindung (jur.)

obligation to disclose assets and income Mitteilungspflicht über Vermögen und Einkommen (soz.)

obligation to report Meldepflicht (med.)

obligatory disposition Mussvorschrift (jur.)

observance Beachtung, Befolgung

observation Beobachtung, Bemerkung, Überwachung

observer Beobachter/in

obsessional neurosis Zwangsneurose (psych.)

obsession Zwang (psych.), Zwangsvorstellung

obsessive zwanghaft (psych.)

occupation Beschäftigung

occupational disease Berufskrankheit

occupational healthcare Arbeitsmedizin

occupational pension Betriebsrente

occupational therapy Beschäftigungstherapie (psych.)

occupier Bewohner/in

odd job Gelegenheitsarbeit

offender Straftäter/in

offer proof Beweis antreten

office duty Innendienst (Sozialarbeiter)

official Beamter, Beamtin 🕮 Beamtentum

official guardian Amtsvormund

official note Bescheid (adm.)

official secret Amtsgeheimnis, Dienstgeheimnis

old age assistance (USA) Altenhilfe (Geldleistung)

old age pension (OAP) Altersruhegeld

ombudsman Beauftragter (z.B. Kinderschutz, Krankenhauswesen)

ommission Auslassung, Versäumnis

on-call dienstbereit

one-dimensional eindimensional

once-off payment einmalige Zahlung (Abfindung, Beihilfe)

one-parent benefit (UK) erhöhtes Kindergeld für allein Erziehende

one-parent family Einelternfamilie

on-the-job training Ausbildung am Arbeitsplatz

open-door provisions offene Hilfe (jun., sen.)

operating costs Betriebskosten

operational competence Handlungskompetenz

operational funktionsfähig

opinion Meinung

opportune opportun, günstig, passend

opportunity Gelegenheit

ordinance Verordnung (jur.)

organisation Leitung (Veranstaltung)

organiser Organisator, "Kalender und Tagebuch“

orphans pension Waisenrente

orthodox orthodox

orthodoxy Rechtgläubigkeit

orthopaedic aids orthopädische Hilfsmittel

orthopedagogic foster places heilpädagogische Pflegestelle

orthopedagogical institutions heilpädagogische Einrichtungen

ostracise ächten

other Andere(r)

outcome Ergebnis

out-going kontaktfreudig

out-group Fremdgruppe (soziol.)

outing Ausflug

out-patient care ambulante Versorgung (med.)

out-patient services extramurale (gemeindenahe psychiatrische) Versorgung

out-patient treatment ambulante Behandlung

outpost Vorposten

outputs Ertrag

outrage Gräueltat, Verbrechen, jemanden empören

out-reach Kontaktaufnahme (soz.), aufsuchend

out-reach (social) work aufsuchende Sozialarbeit (Straßensozialarbeit, Hausbesuche)

outsider Außenseiter/in

overall plan Gesamtplan

overall provision allgemeine Daseinsvorsorge (der Gemeinden)

overcrowded überbelegt (Wohnung, Heim)

overspill (demoskopische) Überflutung

oversupply Überangebot

overtake überholen

owner Eigentümer/in

owner occupier Eigennutzer

own-home child care (USA) Kinderbetreuung zu Hause

– P –

paediatric nurse Kinderkrankenschwester

paediatrician Kinderarzt, Kinderärztin

paradigm Paradigma

paramount of paramount importance von allergrößter Bedeutung

parent education Elternbildung

parent participation Elternbeteiligung (USA: auch Mitwirkung an der Erteilung des Schulunterrichts)

parental authority Elternrecht

parental duty of supervision elterliche Aufsichtspflicht

parenting Betreuung durch Eltern (bes. Kleinkinder), oft verwendet im Zusammenhang mit anderen Begriffen wie parenting skills Betreuungsfähigkeit, parenting course Kurs für Eltern u.ä.), ⇒ child minding

parenting programme Familienbildung (Elternschule)

parents-teachers association Eltern-Lehrerbeirat einer Schule

parish (UK) Landgemeinde, Gemeinde (auch als Kirchengemeinde)

parity Parität

parliament Volksvertretung (i.w.S.), verfassungsgemäß: Parliament

parole Bewährung bei vorzeitiger Haftentlassung

paroxysm Anfall (med.)

partial guardianship Pflegschaft (Personen) (jur.)

partial pension Teilrente

partial session kleine Kammer (Gericht)

participant Teilnehmer

participation Teilnahme

participatory teilnahmeorientiert, teilnehmend

participatory democracy Beteiligungsdemokratie

participatory design einbeziehende, offene Planungsarbeit

participatory evaluation teilnehmende Beobachtung

participatory workshop organisierter offener Erfahrungsaustausch

partner Partner/in

partnership Partnerschaft

partnership, social ~ Sozialpartnerschaft

pass on a file zuschreiben (Vorgang)

passive passiv

passivity Passivität

patch social work feldorientierte Sozialarbeit

patch-social work team Gruppe von Sozialarbeitern und Hilfskräften in feldorientierter Arbeitsweise

paternity trial Vaterschaftsprozess (jur.)

paternity Vaterschaft

pathological krankhaft

patient Patient/in (med.)

patient days Pflegetage (Krankenhaus)

patriarchal patriarchalisch

patriarchy Patriarchat

patron Schirmherr, Stammgast

patronage Schirmherrschaft, Förderung

patronizing herablassend

pattern of behaviour Verhaltensweise

pauperism Verarmung ganzer Schichten und Generationen

pay-off Abfindung (bei Beendigung eines Arbeitsverhältnisses), abzahlen

PAYE (pay as you earn) Lohnsteuer (Arbeitnehmer)

payment Zahlung

payment by installments Abzahlung

payroll tax Lohnsummensteuer (Betrieb)

pedagogy Pädagogik

peer-group Gleichaltrige, Gleichgestellte

peer education Erziehung durch Gleichaltrige

peer learning Lernen in der Gruppe Gleichgesinnter

peer pressure Gruppenzwang (in der Gruppe Gleichgesinnter)

peer support Unterstützung der Altersgenossen

penal code Strafgesetzbuch

penal register Strafregister

penalty Strafe

penalty of imprisonment Freiheitsstrafe (jur.)

penitentiary (USA) Strafanstalt, Zuchthaus, Besserungsanstalt (veraltet)

penology Strafrecht (als Wissenschaft)

pension Ruhegehalt, Rente, Versorgung

pension off in den Ruhestand versetzen

pent-up aufgestaut, Nachholbedarf

penury äußerste Bedürftigkeit

people Leute, Volk (z.B. auch: the people of Ireland das irische Volk, die irische Bevölkerung)

people's organisations Volksorgansationen, Massenbewegung

people's movements Volksbewegung

percentage Prozentsatz

perception Wahrnehmung

performance Leistung

performance evaluation Leistungsbemessung

permanent case Pflegefall (med.)

permanent nursing care Dauerpflege, Dauerpflegefall, Pflegefall

permission Genehmigung

persecution Verfolgung

person at risk Gefährdete/r

personal care persönliche Betreuung

personal development Persönlichkeitsentwicklung

personal services persönliche Hilfen, Sozialdienst

persons in need of supervision (USA) Kinder, Jugendliche, auch erwachsene Gefährdete, die öffentlicher Hilfen bedürfen bzw. öffentlicher Aufsicht zwangsunterstellt werden

persuit Verfolgung

philanthropy Menschenliebe, wohltätige Vereinigung, Stiftung (veraltet) 📖 Wohlfahrtsverband

physical environment örtliche Umwelt

physician Arzt, Ärztin

pitfall Falle, Fallstrick

pivotal zentral (Problem oder Thema, um das sich alles dreht)

place of residence Wohnsitz

placement Unterbringung (Anstalt, Heim, Pflegestelle), Vermittlung (Heimplatz. Pflegestelle), Fremdplacierung (Familie, Wohngruppe), Praktikum

planning Planung

planning authority Planungshoheit

planning board Planungsamt

planning department Planungsabteilung

planning game Planspiel (i.w.S.)

planning law Planungsrecht

planning permission Planungsgenehmigung

plantiff Kläger (jur.)

pleasure principle Lustprinzip (psych.)

pledge versprechen

plenary-meeting Vollversammlung

plenary-session Plenarsitzung

plight Notlage

police Polizei

policy Politik (Politikbereich)

politics politischer Prozess

polity politische Institution

ponce Zuhälter

popular populär

popularity Beliebtheit

population development Bevölkerungsentwicklung

population growth Bevölkerungszunahme

population influx Zuwanderung (bes. in Städte)

population policy Bevölkerungspolitik

populist Populist/in

portage Beförderungsdienste (sen., jun.)

postal watch Hilfe durch den Briefträger (soz.) (Schweden)

postpone aufschieben, verschieben

postponement Aufschub

poverty Armut

poverty indicators Armutsindikatoren

poverty line Armutsgrenze

poverty trap Armutsfalle

power Macht, Energie, Kompetenz, Schwung 🕮 community

power of attorney Vollmacht

power of signature, power to sign Zeichnungsbefugnis

practical praktisch

practice Praxis

practice teacher Praxisanleiter/in

practician Praktiker/in

practitioner professionelle/r Praktiker/in

precarious unsicher, gefährdet (Lebensumstände), auf Widerruf

precedence Vorrang (Gesetz, Leistungspflicht)

predicament Zwangslage

pre-empt vorherbestimmen, determinieren

pregnancy Schwangerschaft

prejudice Vorurteil

preliminary proceedings Ermittlungsverfahren (jur.)

premises Gelände, Geschäftsräume

pre-school Vorschule (im Kindergarten oder Schulkindergarten)

prescribed offiziell aufgeführt (z.B. Berufskrankheit), verordnet

prescription Verordnung (med.)

prescriptive verordnend

pressure-group Interessengruppe

prevention of accidents Unfallverhütung

prevention Vorsorge (med.), Verhinderung

preventive detention Sicherungsverwahrung

preventive health care Gesundheitsvorsorge

preventive health check Vorsorgeuntersuchung

preventive provisions Vorsorgesystem

preventive vorbeugend, präventiv

primary health care (WHO) Grundversorgung (med.)

privacy Intimsphäre, Privatraum

private agencies freie Träger 🕮 Wohlfahrtsverband

private associations freie Verbände 🕮 Wohlfahrtsverband

private pension betriebliche Altersversorgung

probability Wahrscheinlichkeit

probate gerichtliche Testamentseröffnung (jur.)

probation Bewährung (jur., adm.)

probation officer Bewährungshelfer/in, Sozialarbeiter/in im Justizdienst

probation service Bewährungshilfe

probationer Proband/in

problem user Suchtgefährdete/r

procedure Verfahren (auch: juristisches Verfahren, dann aber oft case)

process Prozess (i.S.v. Ablauf, Vorgang)

procession Prozession, Umzug

procuracy Bevollmächtigung

procurer Zuhälter

professional attendants Pflegekräfte (bes. sen.)

professional carers Helfer (soz.)

professionalisation Professionalisierung, Verberuflichung 🕮 Beamtentum

professionalism Fachlichkeit, Expertentum

proficiency Leistung (persönliche Tüchtigkeit)

profligacy Verschwendungssucht (jur.)

prognosis Prognose (med., sen.)

program development (USA) Programmentwicklung

progress Fortschritt

progressive fortschrittlich

progressive design Planspiel (bes. Sozialplanung)

project Projekt

projected vorgesehen, in Planung

propensity Hang (psych.)

prosecution strafrechtliche Verfolgung

prosecutor Staatsanwalt, Staatsanwältin

prosperity Wohlstand, as well wealth

prosperous wohlhabend

prostitute Prostituierte/r

protected tenancy (UK) Mieterschutz

protection against dismissal Kündigungschutz (bes. Schwerbehinderte, Mütter, Wehrdienstpflichtige)

protection of tenancy Kündigungsschutz im Mietrecht

protection Wahrung (der Interessen des Klienten)

provide versorgen mit (i.S.v. vorsorglich bereitstellen, z.B. Einrichtungen) (soz.)

protest Widerspruch einlegen

protest action Protestaktion

protest movement Protestbewegung

protester Demonstrant/in

proto-type Musterbild

provident fund (UK) Genossenschaftssparkasse, Vorsorgefonds

provident provision private Vorsorge

provident society Unterstützungsverein, Versicherungskasse

provider of finance Finanzierungsträger

providing authority Vorsorgeverwaltung

provision Bereitstellung, Vorsorgemaßnahme

provisions Einrichtungen (Summe aller Angebote) (soz.)

proximity Nähe, Annäherung

psychagogy Psychagogik

psychiatric hospital psychiatrisches Fachkrankenhaus

psychiatrist Psychiater/in

psycho-analyst Psychoanalytiker/in

psychogenic psychogen

psychologist Psychologe, Psychologin

psychosis Psychose, Geisteskrankheit (allgemein)

psychosomatic illness psychosomatische Krankheit

psychotherapist Psychotherapeut/in

public agencies öffentliche Träger 🕮 Wohlfahrtsverband

public assistance office Sozialamt

public forum öffentliches Forum

public health services öffentlicher Gesundheitsdienst

public housing agency (USA) Wohnungsamt

public law öffentliches Recht

public meeting öffentliches Treffen, öffentliche Versammlung

public opinion öffentliche Meinung

public relations Öffentlichkeitsarbeit

public weal Gemeinwohl

public welfare agencies Sozialleistungsträger

public welfare office (USA) Sozialamt

publication Veröffentlichung

publicity öffentliches Aufsehen

publish veröffentlichen

pumping priming öffentliche Gelder für den Start einer privaten Initiative

punishment Strafe

punitive measure Strafmaßname

purchasing power Kaufkraft

purpose bound zweckgebunden (Leistung, Zuwendung)

pusher Drogenhändler/in

– Q –

qualification Qualifikation (beruflich), Einschränkung (einer Feststellung)

qualify anspruchsberechtigt sein, Voraussetzungen erfüllen, einschränken

qualifying period Probezeit (i.S.v. Praktikum), Anwartschaftszeit

qualitiative qualitativ

quantitative quantitativ

quantity Menge

query Anfrage, in Zweifel ziehen

question Frage

questionnaire Fragebogen

– R –

race Rasse, Rassenzugehörigkeit, Rennen, Wettlauf

racism Rassismus

racist abuse rassistischer Missbrauch (körperlicher oder psychischer Angriff, begründet durch Rassismus)

racist attack rassistischer Übergriff

racist language rassistische Sprache

racist practice rassistische Handlungen

radical radikal

radicalise radikalisieren

radicalism Radikalismus

raid Angriff, Razzia; angreifen

railway Eisenbahn

rape Vergewaltigung, vergewaltigen

rapist Vergewaltiger

rapporteur Berichterstatter/in

rate Kurs, Tarif, Grad

rates (UK) Gemeindesteuer

rationale logische Grundlage, rationale Erklärung

rationality Rationalität, Vernunft

rationing Zuteilung (Lebensmittel)

react ansprechen, reagieren

reaction Reaktion

reactionary Reaktionär

reasonable angemessen

rebuke maßregeln (päd.)

recede schwinden

recession Rezession

recidivism Rückfall (jur.)

recipient Empfänger/in

reckon anrechnen, in Ansatz bringen

reckonable anrechnungspflichtig, anrechnungsfähig

recompense Schadensersatz

reconciliation Versöhnung, auch i.S.v. Zusammenführung, e.g. reconciliation of family life and work Zusammenführung von Arbeits- und Privatleben

reconnaissance Aufklärung, Erkundung

record Aufzeichnung, Niederschrift, Akte

recovery Wiederherstellung

recurrence Rückfall (medizinisch)

redistributing administration verteilende Verwaltung

redistribution Umverteilung

reduction Abstrich, Absenkung, Verringerung (Leistungen), Ermäßigung (Eintritt, Beitrag)

reference group Bezugsgruppe

reference Zeugnis (Beruf)

referendum Referendum, Volksentscheid, Volksabstimmung

referral Vermittlung (Heim, Pflegeheim) (sen.), Überweisung, Einweisung

reformatory (USA) Erziehungsanstalt

refuge Asyl, Zufluchtsort

refugee Flüchtling

refuse zurückweisen, ablehnen, Abfall

region Region, Gebiet, Gegend, in the region of etwa, ungefähr

regional regional

register of births, deaths and marriage (UK) Personenstandsregister

register of births, marriages and burials (USA) Personenstandsregister

regulation Regulierung, Regelung, Rechtsverordnung, Gesetz 🕮 law

regulator Regler (technisch), Aufseher (administrativ)

rehabilitation Rehabilitation, Eingliederung

reimbursement Kostenerstattung

re-instatement Wiedereinsetzung in den vorigen Stand

rejection Ablehnung

relapse Rückfall (med.)

relation Beziehung, Verwandte/r

relationship Beziehung, Freundschaft

relative Verwandte/r (⇒ kinship, ⇒ auch sibbling)

release Entlassung (Gefangene), Entbindung (von Pflichten), erlassen (Strafe, Schuld)

released prisoner Strafentlassener

relief Unterstützung

relieve Linderung

reluctant widerwillig

remand custody Untersuchungshaft

remand home Jugendstrafanstalt

remedial education Sonderpädagogik, Förderunterricht

remedial heilend

remedial school Sonderschule

remedy Heilmittel

reminder Mahnschreiben

remonstrate sich beschweren, protestieren

rent allowance ⇒ rent supplement (USA) Mietbeihilfe

rent Miete

rent supplement ergänzende Mietbeihilfe

rent-rebate Mietpreisminderung, Mietpreisnachlass

renumeration Rückzahlung, Erstattung

renunciation Verzicht

repair Reparatur

reparation Reparation, Wiedergutmachung

repeal Aufhebung (eines Gesetzes)

repeat Wiederholen

repercussion Auswirkung

report Beurteilung (Personalakte), Zeugnis (Schule)

reporter Berichterstatter/in

repression Verdrängung (psych.)

repressive repressiv, unterdrückend

request for judicial assistance (UK) Rechtshilfeersuchen (jur.)

reservation Vorbehalt (jur.)

residence permit Aufenthaltserlaubnis

resident wohnhaft, Bewohner/in

residential care Heimerziehung

resident's association Bewohnerversammlung

resident's group Bewohnergruppe

resocialisation Resozialisierung

resource Mittel

resource-centre Gemeindezentrum

resources Hilfsquellen (verfügbare Mittel)

resource person Person, die über Ressourcen verfügt und sie einer Gruppe zur Verfügung stellt, ohne diese zu leiten

respite care Urlaubspflege (bes. Seh- und Behinderte)

respond ansprechen, reagieren

respondent Beklagte/r (bes. bei Scheidung), Antwortende/r

responsibility Zuständigkeit(sbereich), auch: **competency**

responsible in penal law strafrechtliche Verantwortlichkeit

responsive mitteilsam

restitution Wiederherstellung (Zustand Rechtslage), Kostenerstattung (zwischen sozialen Trägern)

restitution of assets and rights Wiedergutmachung

restriction Einschränkung (Leistungen)

restriction of liberty Freiheitsbeschränkung

retarded entwicklungsgestört, zurückgeblieben

retirement Ruhestand

retirement community Seniorensiedlung (bes. USA)

retirement pension Ruhegeld (Pension für Beamte)

retraining Umschulung

retraining subsidies Umschulungsbeihilfe (für Betriebe)

retrial Wiederaufnahmeverfahren (Zivilrecht)

retrenchment Abbau (Arbeitskräfte, Leistungen)

retrial Wiederaufnahmeverfahren (Strafrecht)

revelation Enthüllung, Aufdeckung

review Überprüfung (Unterlagen, Fall)

revile verunglimpfen, schmähen

right of inheritance Erbrecht (persönliches)

right to custody elterliches Sorgerecht

rights Rechte

rising fives Kinder, die noch nicht das fünfte Lebensjahr vollendet haben, aber bereits eingeschult werden

risk Risiko

risk assessment Risikoabschätzung

risk management Risikomanagement

road Straße

road's protest Straßenprotest

role Rolle

role-game Rollenspiel

role-play Rollenspiel

round table discussion Diskussion am Runden Tisch

rural district Landkreis (adm.)

– S –

safe place Jugendschutzstelle

safebuarding Absicherung (Anspruch)

scarce knapp

school nurture group intensive Schulsozialarbeit mit geschädigten oder benachteiligten Kindern (soz.)

scope for judgement Beurteilungsspielraum

search Durchsuchung

secrecy Schweigepflicht (jur.)

section-1-Assistance Sozialhilfe nach Ermessen (nur bei Gefährdung von Kindern)

secure place sicherer Ort (geschlossene Anstalt)

seeing-eye dog (USA) Blindenhund

seize s.th. (v.) pfänden (Gegenstände des Eigentums)

self administration Selbstverwaltung (Gemeinden)

self-appreciation Selbsteinschätzung

self-awareness Selbsterfahrung (psych.)

self-commitment Selbstbindung (Gremien)

self-concept Selbstbild (psych.)

self consciousness Verlegenheit (allg.), Selbstbewusstsein (philos., psych.)

selfgovernment Selbstverwaltung (Körperschaft)

self-harm Selbstschädigung

self-help Selbsthilfe

self-management Selbstverwaltung (soz.)

self-realisation Selbstfindung (psych.)

senescence Altern (biol., med.)

sense of community Gemeinsinn

sensory disablement Sinnesbehinderung

separation Trennung (auch von Partner- u. Ehebeziehungen)

sequel in court gerichtliches Nachspiel, Folgeerscheinung

sequela Spätfolge (med., soz.)

serenity Gelassenheit

setting Rahmenbedingungen, Umgebung (i.S.v. Hintergrund)

settlement Vergleich (jur.), Siedlung

sex Geschlecht (biol.) ⇒ gender

sexually transmitted disease (WHO) Geschlechtskrankheit (med.)

sheaf Bündel, Bündelung von Maßnahmen

sheltered housing betreutes Wohnen (Behinderte und Sen.)

sheltered workshop beschützende Werkstatt, Werkstatt für Behinderte

shopping basket ⇒ bread basket

short-coming Unzulänglichkeit

short-fall Fehlbetrag, Fehlbestand

short-time work Kurzarbeit (nicht unbedingt im Sinne der deutschen Gesetzgebung)

sibling Geschwister ⇒ kinship ⇒ relative

sick benefit Krankenhilfe (soz.)

sick pay Lohnfortzahlung (bei Krankheit)

sick ward Krankenstation

sickness benefit (UK) Krankengeld

sickness Krankheit

side-effect Nebenwirkung

sign language Gebärdensprache (Minderheitensprache, nicht zu verwechseln mit einer "technischen Hilfssprache") 📖 sign language

single allein stehend

single parent allein erziehender Elternteil

skilled workers gelernte Arbeiter (Facharbeiter)

social sozial, gemeinschaftlich

social audit Sozialbudget

social centre Sozialstation, insb. als Begegnungsstätte

social class Schicht (soz.)

social contract Generationenvertrag

social contributions (UK) Sozialabgaben (Sozialbeiträge)

social control soziale Kontrolle (i.e.S., über und durch die Gesellschaft)

social court (D) Sozialgericht

social establishment soziale Einrichtung

social functioning soziales Funktionieren (Bewältigung des Lebens in der Gesellschaft)

social fund Hilfsfonds (für Härtefälle)

social group work soziale Gruppenarbeit

social health services Gesundheitshilfe

social income Sozialeinkommen

social insurance Sozialversicherung

social justice soziale Gerechtigkeit

social maladjustement Verwahrlosung (Erwachsene)

social network Beziehungsgeflecht

social paediatrics Sozialpädiatrie

social pedagogics Sozialpädagogik

social pedagogue Sozialpädagoge, Sozialpädagogin

social perception soziale Wahrnehmung

social planning Sozialplanung

social policy Sozialpolitik

social provisions soziale Infrastruktur (vorhandene Angebote), Sozialleistungen (i.w.S.)

social psychiatry Sozialpsychiatrie

social psychology Sozialpsychologie

social safety net soziales Netz

social sciences Sozialwissenschaften

social security soziale Sicherheit (USA, meist nur für Altersrentenversicherung gebräuchlich)

social service centre Sozialstation, orientiert auf persönliche Dienstleistungen

social skills training soziales Training (insbes. für junge Rechtsbrecher)

social support system Hilfssystem

social tax (USA) Sozialbeitrag

social therapist Sozialtherapeut/in

social therapy Sozialtherapie

social welfare Fürsorgewesen (Sozialleistungszahlungen, Sozialleistungssystem)

social welfare assistance Sozialhilfe

social work Sozialarbeit (professionell) 📖 social intervention

social worker Sozialarbeiter/in

socialisation Sozialisation

socially incompetent dissozial (psych.)

societal gemeinschaftlich

sociology Soziologie

solatium Schmerzensgeld

solicitor Rechtsanwalt/Rechtsanwältin (nur bei niedrigen Gerichten zugelassen) ⇒ advocate

solidarity Solidarität, Zusammengehörigkeitsgefühl, Gemeinschaftsverbundenheit

source country Entsendeland, Herkunftsland (Einwanderer, Flüchtlinge usw.)

spa Heilbad, Kurbad

special representative Vertrauensmann (für Schwerbehinderte im Betrieb)

special school (UK) Sonderschule (päd.)

speech impediment (WHO) Sprachbehinderung

spill-over überlaufen, auf einen anderen Bereich sich ausbreitend

sponsor Förderer

spouse abuse Gewalttätigkeit gegen Ehegatten

spouse Ehegatte/Ehegattin

scrutinise genau prüfen, mustern

staff council Personalrat

staff system Stabssystem (adm.) (funktionale Beteiligung an Leitungsaufgaben, mit formaler Anweisungsbefugnis oder beratend)

standard benefits einheitliche Leistungen

standard value Richtwert (Planung)

standing rules Satzung (freie Verbände)

state for the minutes zu Protokoll geben

statement Feststellung (Aussage)

stationary stationär

status offender Jugendliche, die Schutzbestimmungen oder Schulpflicht verletzen (USA)

statute Satzung (Organisation, Gemeinde)

statutory body öffentliche Einrichtung

statutory duty Rechtspflicht

statutory forced share (USA) Pflichtteil

statutory guardianship Amtsvormundschaft, Amtspflegschaft

statutory health insurance fund gesetzliche Krankenkasse

statutory health insurance gesetzliche Krankenversicherung

statutory instrument (UK) Rechtsverordnung

statutory insurance Pflichtversicherung

statutory law niedergelegtes Recht (Gegensatz: Gewohnheitsrecht)

statutory offence Straftat

statutory sick pay (SSP) (UK) gesetzliche Lohnfortzahlung im Krankheitsfalle

step child Stiefkind

step parents Stiefeltern

steward Ordner (z.B. bei Demonstrationen)

stipulate zur Auflage machen, vereinbaren

strange seltsam

stranger Fremde/r 🕮 Ausländer

stratum soziale Schicht

stream (UK) Leistungsstufe (Parallelzug) (päd)

street people Stadtstreicher/in, Obdachlose

street work Straßensozialarbeit 🕮 social intervention

stress test Belastungserprobung (Behinderte), Belastungstest (med.)

student on placement Praktikant/in

subculture Subkultur

subject to approval genehmigungspflichtig

subsidised housing Sozialwohnungen (insgesamt)

subsidised housing construction sozialer Wohnungsbau (mit öffentlichen Mitteln durch Private)

subsistence Lebensunterhalt (Mindest-, Regelbedarf)

substandard nicht den Mindestanforderungen entsprechend (z.B. Wohnverhältnisse)

success Erfolg

successive aufeinanderfolgend

succour Beistand, Hilfe

suffer leiden

sufficient ausreichend, genügend

summons Vorladung

superannuated person Ruhegeldempfänger

superannuation Ruhegeld

superior Vorgesetzte/r

supersede ablösen (neues Gesetz das frühere)

superstructure Überbau

supervised apartment Altenwohnung

supervision Supervision

supervision in probation Bewährungsaufsicht

supervision of conduct Führungsaufsicht

supervision order Betreuungsweisung

supervisor Supervisor/in

supplement ergänzende soziale Leistung (z.B. in Härtefällen)

supplemental feeding program for women, infants and children – WIC (USA) Nahrungsmittelhilfe

supplemental security income (USA) Zusatzleistung der Sozialhilfe zu niedrigsten Altersrenten

supplementary benefit (UK) Sozialhilfe für Alleinstehende

support (USA) Alimente

supportive education Fördererziehung (päd.)

supportive measures unterstützende Maßnahmen

surrogate family Ersatzfamilie

surrogate mother Leihmutter

surroundings Umgebung (räumlich)

surveillance Überwachung (gefährdeter alter Menschen oder Kinder)

survey Erhebung (stat.)

surviving dependent Hinterbliebene/r

survivor's benefit (UK) Hinterbliebenenrente (wenn zeitlich begrenzt)

survivor's pension Hinterbliebenenrente

suspend aussetzen, vorübergehend einstellen (von Zahlungen, eines Verkaufes ...)

suspended sentence Bewährungsstrafe

suspension Einstellung (Verfahren)

suspension of execution Vollstreckungsaufschub

suspension of sentence Strafaussetzung

swab Abstrich (med.)

synergy Zusammenwirken

– T –

take-up (rate) Nutzungsgrad (Angebote, zustehende Leistungen)

target-group Zielgruppe

targeting Zielgruppenausrichtung

task-force Sondereinheit, Spezialeinheit, mit einer besonderen Aufgabe betreute Gruppe

tax-allowance Steuerfreibetrag

tax-break Steuergrenze

tax-credit Steuerfreibetrag

tax examption Steuerbefreiung

tax liability Steuerpflichtigkeit

taxing belastend (psych.)

technical college Fachschule, Fachhochschule

teen-age mother jugendliche Mutter (unter 20 Jahren)

teen-age pregnancy Schwangerschaft (bei unter 20-Jährigen)

tee-totaller Abstinenzler/in

telephone reassurance Telefonkette

telephone service help line Telefonhilfen

temporary disability payment (USA) Krankengeld (Privatversicherung oder Arbeitgeber)

temporary disablement compensation (USA) Krankengeld (s.S.)

temporary guardian Pfleger/in (jur.)

temporary insanity Bewusstseinsstörung (jur.)

temporary shelter Notunterbringung

temporary worker Leiharbeiter/in, Arbeiter/in auf Zeit

tenancy Miete, Mietverhältnis

tenant Mieter/in

tenant protection Mieterschutz

tendency Anlage (psych., päd.)

tending Betreuung hilfloser oder abhängiger Personen

term, full normale Schwangerschaftsdauer (med.)

terminal aid Sterbehilfe

terminal care Sterbebegleitung, -pflege

terminal illness unheilbare Krankheit

termination of pregnancy Schwangerschaftsabbruch

therap(eut)ist Therapeut/in

therapeutic community therapeutische Wohngemeinschaft

therapeutic day care centre Kindertagesstätte mit Familientherapie

therapeutic education Heilerziehung (psych., päd.)

therapeutic educator Heilpädagoge, Heilpädagogin

therapeutical group home therapeutische Wohngruppe

third-party pension Fremdrente

throw-away society Wegwerfgesellschaft

time-limit Frist

time off Dienstbefreiung (adm.), Freizeit

toddler Kleinkind (im Krabbelalter)

total institution totale Institution

town and country planning Regionalplanung

township (USA) Leistungsstufe (Parallelzug) (päd.)

trafficking illegal Handel treiben

traineeship Praktikum

training centre (UK) Rehabilitationszentrum (soz.)

tramp Landstreicher (eher abwertend)

transformation durchgreifender Wandel

transition Übergang

transition payment Übergangsgeld (s.S.)

transition phase Übergangsphase

transitional home Übergangseinrichtung, Übergangsheim

transnational international (grenzüberschreitend)
📖 international

transportation aid technische Fortbewegungshilfe (für Behinderte)

transportation allowance Beförderungszuschuss (soz.)

transportation services Fahrdienste (für Behinderte)

trap Falle

Travellers' Aid Society, passenger aid, passenger aid on the railway station Bahnhofsmission 🕮 traveller

Treat behandeln (allgemein und ebenso im medizinischen Sinn)

treatment behandeln, Behandlung (allgemein und ebenso im medizinischen Sinn)

treatment centre Behandlungszentrum, Erziehungsanstalt (UK)

trial period Probezeit (i.w.S.)

trial Prozess (jur.)

trial stay Probewohnen (sen.)

tribunal Untersuchungsausschuss, Tribunal

trouble Ärger, Sorge, Umstände machen

truant Schulschwänzer/in

trusteeship Pflegschaft (Vermögen), Beistandschaft (jur.)

turnover Umsatz, Zu- und Abgänge (Personal, Klienten)

tutoring (USA) Hausaufgabenhilfe

– U –

umbrella-organisation Dachorganisation

unconstitutional verfassungswidrig

undertaking bindende Zusage

underworld Unterwelt, Halbwelt

undocumented workers (USA) illegale, ausländische Arbeiter

uneconomical (behaviour) unwirtschaftlich(es Verhalten)

unemployed erwerbslos

unemployment Erwerbslosigkeit

unemployment benefit (UK) Erwerbslosigkeitsgeld (s.S.)

unification Vereinheitlichung, Einheitsbildung

university Universität

use value Gebrauchswert

utilise benutzen

utilisation Nutzung (sozialer Angebote)

– V –

vagrancy Landstreicherei

vagrant Obdachtlose/r, Landstreicher/in 🕮 traveller

validity Rechtskraft

value added tax (VAT) Mehrwertsteuer

vested interest persönliches Interesse

vested interests Interessengruppen

viable lebensfähig, durchführbar

vicinity Nachbarschaft (physische, auch im übertragenen Sinn)

vigil Nachtwache

violation of rule, law, agreement Verstoß gegen Vorschrift, Gesetz, Vereinbarung

violence Gewalttätigkeit

violence prone zur Gewalttätigkeit neigend (psych.)

visiting health work aufsuchende Gesundheitsversorgung

visiting nurse Gemeindeschwester

visiting resident program (USA) Probewohnen (sen.)

vocational capability Berufsfähigkeit

voluntary insurance freiwillige Versicherung

volunteer Freiwillige/r (Helfer/in) (soz.)

vote (v.) abstimmen (wählen)

voters registration Wahlregistrierung

voucher Gutschein (generell, auch z.B. für Naturalleistungen, USA: bes. Lebensmittel)

vulnerable (sozial) schwach, verletzlich

– W –

wage-tax Lohnsteuer (Arbeitnehmer)

wages council (UK) Schiedsstelle (Lohnverhandlungen), Gremium zur Festsetzung von Mindestlöhnen

wait-and-see attitude abwartende Haltung

waiting period Wartezeit

waiver Verzichterklärung (jur.)

walk of life sozialer Status, auch situationsbezogen: Lebenssituation, Lebensumstände

walking the streets auf den Strich gehen

war blind Kriegsblinde

war disabled person Kriegsbeschädigte/r

war pensions administration Versorgungsamt (Kriegsopfer)

war victim Kriegsopfer

ward Mündel (jur.), Krankenstation, Wahlbezirk

ward of the state Kind in Fürsorgeerziehung (Elternrecht auf Behörde übertragen)

warden Heimleiter/in, Aufseher/in (z.B. auch dog-warden, litter-warden)

wardship Vormundschaft

warrant Haftbefehl, Rechtfertigung, etwas rechtfertigen

watching Beobachtung

weigh gewichten

welfare Jugendpflege, Jugendhilfe, Jugendfürsorge, Wohlfahrt, Fürsorge(-tätigkeit)

welfare-industry (USA) kommerzielle Sozial- oder Gesundheitsdienste, Einrichtungen

welfare law Sozialrecht

welfare machinery Infrastruktur im Sozialbereich (Sachinvestitionen, Organisationen)

welfare recipient Hilfeempfänger, insbesondere mit Blick auf "harte Leistungen", rechtlich zustehende Leistungen

welfare rights soziale Rechtsansprüche (jur.)

welfare state Wohlfahrtsstaat

welfare worker Sozialarbeiter/in in der Jugendhilfe

wheelchair (user) Rollstuhl(fahrer/in)

widow's allowance Witwengeld (für begrenzte Zeit)

widowed mother's allowance Kinderzuschlag zur Witwenrente

widower's pension Witwerrente

widows pension Witwenrente

withdraw zurückziehen (auch administrativ, finanziell etc.)

withdrawn kontaktarm (psych.)

women's (liberation) movement Frauenbewegung

Women's Aid Centre Frauenhaus

women's concerns Frauenfragen

women's refuge Frauenhaus

work (or employment contract) Arbeitsvertrag

work shy (obsolete) arbeitsscheu (veraltet)

worker's compensation Erwerbsunfähigkeitsrente

workfare programs (USA) Verbindung von Sozialhilfe mit Arbeits- und Ausbildungsangeboten

working group Arbeitsgemeinschaft

working party Arbeitsgruppe

workman's compensation (USA) betriebliche Unfallversicherung

workplace Arbeitsplatz

works constitution Betriebsverfassung

writ Erlass

writ of execution Vollstreckungsbefehl

– X –

xenophobia Fremdenfeindlichkeit

– Y –

young person jung, jugendlich (soz.) (UK) 14- bis 17-jährige (jur.)

youth Jugendliche, Jugend

youth board (USA) lokaler Bürgerausschuss für Jugendhilfe (freiwillig)

youth development Jugendförderung

youth enablement Hilfe beim Übergang zum Erwachsensein

youth gang Jugendbande

youth hostel Jugendherberge

Youth Opportunities Programme (YOP) (UK) Arbeit und Ausbildung für jugendliche Arbeitslose

Youth Service Bureau (USA) lokale, oft mit Schule oder Polizei zusammenarbeitende Dienststelle, die auf erziehungsschwierige Minderjährige ohne Anrufung von Gerichten einwirkt

Youth Training Scheme (UK) Jugend-ausbildungsprogramm (Arbeitslose)

Appendices

Gesetze, Organisationen/Institutionen, offizielle Begriffe, Begriffe aus Gesetzen etc.

Laws and Regulations, Organisations/Institutions, official terms, terms used in laws etc.

Abschlagzahlung advance payment

Act on the payment of Child Raising Benefit and Child Raising Leave Ausbildungsförderungsgesetz

Adoptionsgesetz Adoption Act

Adoptionsvermittlungsgesetz Law concerning the mediation of adoptions

Allgemeiner Sozialdienst general social service, neighbourhood team

Amtsblatt official journal

Amtseid official oath

Amtsvormund official guardian

Angestelltenversicherungsgesetz Employees' Insurance Act

Anhörungsrecht employer's right to be heard

Arbeitgeberhaftung employer's liability

Arbeitsauflösungsvereinbarung agreement on the termination of an employment relationship

Arbeitsförderungsgesetz Employment Promotion Act

Arbeitsgesetz labour law

Ausländergesetz Foreigners Act

Baugesetzbuch Construction Code

Bausparkasse building society

Beschäftigungspflicht duty to employ (disabled) people

Betäubungsmittelgesetz Drugs Act; Narcotics Act

Betriebsrat works council

Betriebsrente company pension

Bundesangestelltentarifvertrag – BAT federal collective agreement for employees of the public sector

Bundesanstalt für Arbeit Federal Institute for Employment, Federal Employment services

Bundesanstalt für Arbeit, Neutralität der neutrality of the Federal Institute for Employment

Bundesarbeitsgericht Federal Labour Court

Bundesausbildungsförderungsgesetz Federal Educational Grants Act

Bundesbank Federal Bank

Bundeserziehungsgeld- und -erziehungsurlaubsgesetz Federal Law concerning child benefits and parental leave (within the first 12 months of a child's life)

Bundesgerichtshof Federal Court

Bundeskindergeldgesetz Federal Child Benefit Act

Bundesseuchengesetz Federal Epidemics Act

Bundessozialhilfegesetz Federal Public Welfare Act; Social Assistance Act (USA)

Bundesversorgungsgesetz Federal War Victims Relief Act

Bürgerliches Gesetzbuch Civil Code

Christlicher Verein junger Frauen/Männer Young women's Christian Association/Young Men's Christian Association

Datenschutzgesetz (Federal) Data Protection Act

Deutscher Gewerkschaftsbund German Trade Union Congress

Deutsches Rotes Kreuz German Red Cross

EAPN European Anti Poverty Network

Eckregelsatz basic standard rates of social assistance

Entwicklungsprogramm der Vereinten Nationen United Nations Development Programme (UNDP)

Ernährungs- und Landwirtschaftsorganisation der Vereinten Nationen Food and Agriculture Organisation of the United Nations (FAO)

Erziehungsurlaub child raising leave, educational leave

ESAN European Social Action Network

ETUC European Trade Union Congress

Europäische Gemeinschaft European Community

Europäische Union European Union

<u>**Europarat** Council of Europe</u>

Konvention des Europarates zum Schutze der Menschenrechte und Grundfreiheiten (1950) convention of the Council of Europe for the Protection of Human Rights and Fundamental Freedoms (1950)
Europäische Menschenrechtskonvention (1953) European Convention on Human Rights (1953)
Europäisches Fürsorgeabkommen (1953) European Convention on Social and Medical Assistance (1953)
Europäisches Niederlassungsabkommen (1955) European Convention on Establishment (1955)
Haager Minderjährigen-Schutzabkommen (1961) Hague Convention on the protection of Minors (1961)
Europäische Konvention der sozialen Sicherheit European Convention on Social Security
Europäische Konvention über die Adoption von Kindern (1973) European convention on the Adoption of Children (1973)

FEANTSA féderation européenne d' associations nationales travaillant avec les sans- abri/European Federation of National Organizations working with the Homeless/Europäisches Netzwerk von Nationalen Organisationen, die im Bereich Wohnungslosigkeit aktiv sind

flexible Arbeitszeit flexible working hours

Fonds der Vereinten Nationen für die Aktivitäten auf dem Gebiet der Bevölkerung United Nations Fund for Population Activities (UNFPA)

Forschungsinstitut der Vereinten Nationen für soziale Entwicklung United Nations Research Institute for Social Development (UNRISD)

Geschäftsgeheimnis business secret

Gesetz über die Verbreitung jugengefährdender Schriften Act concerning the Distribution of publications Harmuful to Young Persons

Grundgesetz Basic Law (Constitution of the FRG)

Hauptabteilung für internationale Wirtschafts- und Sozialangelegenheiten der Vereinten Nationen United Nations Department of International Economic and Social Affairs (DIESA)

Heimgesetz Homes Act

Internationale Arbeitsorganisation (IAO) - International Labour Organisation (ILO)

Übereinkommen 2 über Arbeitslosigkeit (1919) convention 2 concerning unemployment (1919)
Übereinkommen 29 über Zwangs- oder Pflichtarbeit (1925) Convention 209 concerning forced or compulsory labour (1925)
Übereinkommen 87 über die Vereinigungsfreiheit und den Schutz des Vereinigungsrechtes (1948) convention 87 concerning freedom of association and protection of the right to organize (1948)
Übereinkommen 102 über die Mindestnormen sozialer Sicherheit (1952) convention 102 concerning minimum standards of social security (1952)
Übereinkommen 105 über die Abschaffung der Zwangsarbeit (1957) convention 105 concerning the abolution of forced labour (1957)
Übereinkommen 111 über die Diskriminierung in Beschäftigung und Beruf (1958) convention 11 concerning discrimination in respect of employment and occuption (1958)
Übereinkommen 117 über die grundlegenden Ziele und Normen der Sozialpolitik (1962) Convention 117 concerning basic aims and standards of social policy (1962)
Übereinkommen 118 über die Gleichbehandlung von Inländern und Ausländern in der sozialen Sicherheit (1962) convention 118 concerning equality of treatment of nationals and non-nationals in social security (1962)
Übereinkommen 122 über die Beschäftigungspolitik (1964) Convention 122 concerning employment policy (1964)

Internationale Gesellschaft für die Rehabilitation Behinderter International Society for Rehabilitation of the Handicapped

Internationale Union der Familienorganisationen (IUFO) International Union of Family Organizations (IUFO)

Internationale Vereinigung der Schulen für Sozialarbeit International Association of Schools of Social Work (IASSW)

Internationale Vereinigung für Gerontologie International Association for Gerontology

Internationale Vereinigung für Jugendhilfe International Association for Youth Welfare

Internationale Vereinigung für Soziale Sicherheit (IVSS) ⇒ International Social Security Association (ISSA)

Internationale Vereinigung für Sozialen Fortschritt (IVSF) International Association for Social Progress (IASP)

Internationaler Ausschuss für Wanderungsbewegungen International Committee for Migration (ICM)

Internationaler Gemeindeverband (IGV) International Union of Local Authorities (IULA)

Internationaler Jugendgemeinschaftsdienst (IJGD) International Youth Community Services

Internationaler Rat der Hauspflegedienste International Council of Home Help Services

Internationaler Rat für soziale Wohlfahrt (ICSW) International Council on Social Welfare (ICSW)

Internationaler Sozialdienst (ISD) ⇒ International Social Service (ISS)

Internationaler Verband der Diakonie International Federation of Diaconates

Internationaler Verband der Sozialarbeiter und Sozialpädagogen International Federation of Social Workers (IFSW)

Internationales Arbeiterhilfswerk International Workers Assistance Programme

Internationales Büro gegen Alkoholismus und Suchtgefahren International Council on Alcohol and Addictions (ICAA)

Jugendarbeitsschutzgesetz Law concerning the protection of minors at work.

Jugendegerichtsgesetz Juvenile Court Act

Jugendschutzgesetz Act Protecting Youth in Public

Jugendwohlfahrtsgesetz Youth Welfare Act

Kinderhilfswerk der Vereinten Nationen United Nations Children's Fund (UNICEP)

Kriegsgefangenenentschädigungsgesetz Act on the Indenmification of Prisoners of War

Opferentschädigungsgesetz Act on the Indemnification of Victims of Crime

Raumordnungsgesetz Town and Country Planning Act

Rechtsberatung legal advice

Rechtsberatungsgesetz Act on Legal Advice

Schlichtungsausschuss conciliation committee

Umweltprogramm der Vereinten Nationen United Nations Environment Programme (UNEP)

Verbindungsstelle der Vereinten Nationen zu freien Verbänden United Nations Non-Governmental Liaison Service (NGLS)

Vereinte Nationen (VN)
United Nations (UN)

Allgemeine Erklärung der Menschenrechte (1948) Universal Declaration of Human Rights (1948)
Erklärung der Rechte des Kindes (1959) Declaration of the Rights of the Child (1959)
Abkommen zur Vermeidung von Staatenlosigkeit (1961) Convention on Reduction of Statelessness (1961)

Internationaler Pakt über bürgerliche und politische Rechte (1966) International Convention on Civil and Political Rights (1966)
Internationaler Pakt über wirtschaftliche, soziale und kulturelle Rechte (1966) International Convention on Economic, Social and Cultural Rights (1966)

Verordnung über die soziale Sicherheit der Wanderarbeiter (1971) Regulation on Social Security for Migrant Workers (1971)

Weltbund für seelische Gesundheit World Federation for Mental Health

Weltgesundheitsorganisation (WGO) World Health Organisation (WHO)

Weltgewerkschaftsbund (WGB) World Federation of Trade Unions (WFTU)

Welthandels- und Entwicklungskonferenz der Vereinten Nationen United Nations Conference on Trade and Development (UNCTAD)

Welthungerhilfe World Hunger Aid

Weltverband der Arbeitnehmer (WVA) World Confederation of Labour (WCL)

Wirtschafts- und Sozialrat der Vereinten Nationen United Nations Economic and Social Council (ECOSOC)

Zentrum für Menschenrechte der Vereinten Nationen United Nations Centre for Human Rights

Zentrum für soziale Entwicklung und humanitäre Angelegenheiten der Vereinten Nationen United Nations Centre for Social Development and Humanitarian Affairs

Glossary

ACCESSION CRITERIA

The accession criteria had been had been decided upon at the Copenhagen summit in 1993. They are basically as follows:

the requirement for politically stable, democratic institutions;

the existence of an economic system on the basis of the market;

the incorporation of the ⇒ Community acquis.

AGING

Even if the term is first and foremost concerned with the biological process, the term gained in the meantime a second meaning. In this – additional – view we find a shift from the view on the individual process of getting older to the matter of a changing age structure of the society. This is, in many cases, suggested as negative and "unsustainable".

ARCHITECTURE

The term architecture and as well the term arts had been included to mark a particular trend in community work. We find the development of specific features that have their own character. In this respect architecture plays for example an important part in respect of rural and urban development. In such contexts architecture is not reduced on issues of architecture in a reductionist understanding of building. Rather it serves as a kind of "methodological approach" which includes aspects of spatial planning under the perspective of community development. The same holds true for arts. Actually we find in this area already a particular paradigm of community arts – an approach where arts is not solely a means or method of community development and where, on the other side, community development is not simply a field to which arts is delivered. Rather, community arts is to some extent an own methodological approach of community development, founding a fusion between arts and community work with an new, own quality.

Animation is somewhat linked. However, it is more concerned with the individual and group level whereas architecture and community arts are concerned with the social and societal, i.e. ⇒ community level.

We can find similar developments in other areas and to mention it here is important to mark a trend of further specialisation in the professional development.

AUSLÄNDER

Der Begriff wird im Englischen mit verschiedenen Übersetzungen angegeben. Wenngleich alle "politisch korrekt" – also nicht diskriminierend – sind, sind die Bedeutungen graduell unterschiedlich.

non-national ist die wohl neutralste, politisch-rechtlich begründete Bezeichnung für Menschen, die in einem Land leben, ohne die jeweilige Staatsangehörigkeit zu besitzen. Dies bedeutet auch, dass mit dem Erwerb der Staatsangehörigkeit dieser Status aufgehoben ist.

foreigner meint Personen, die aus einem anderen Land kommen, hat einen ähnlichen Bezug wie *non-national,* aber verbindet dies stark mit dem politisch-sozio-kulturellen Aspekt: Man bleibt *foreigner,* auch wenn man *national citizen* wird.

alien hat tendenziell einen negativen Beigeschmack, ohne aber direkt diskriminierend zu sein. Der Begriff bezieht sich stark auf soziokulturelle Aspekte und verbindet diese mit der Zuordnung zu einem – jeweils gegebenen oder vorgängigen – Ausländer-Status.

stranger ist in gewissem Sinn doppeldeutig, bezieht sich sowohl auf Fremdheit im Nationalitäten-Sinn wie auf Fremdheit in jeglicher anderen Dimension. Die Doppeldeutigkeit besteht darin, dass es sowohl diskriminierend als auch positiv-anerkennend, Neugierde ausdrückend oder auch schlicht objektiv-feststellend sein kann, jemanden als *strang(er)* zu bezeichnen. Der Bezug hier ist in jedem Fall nicht (staats-)rechtlicher Art, sondern bezieht sich auf die Lebensweise. Er ist auch zweiseitig, denn der Fremde in diesem Sinn erscheint nicht nur fremd, sondern fühlt sich auch fremd, ist in fremder Umgebung bzw. unter Fremden.

BEAMTENTUM

E: A brief remark is appropriate regarding the status of the official, the *Beamte* as this position (a) concerns a large group of employees concerned with social (welfare) issues who are (b) specifically located in the social order. As specific as this position is as specific it is for the German system, as we find in particular there regulations on the

* limited possibility of job termination by the employer
* peculiarities of income, taxation, social security etc.
* a particular liability to loyalty and execute statutory tasks with full neglect of personal attitudes and interests.

This is founded in the view of the commitment of complete obligation of the official to the state. This is not seen as duty to fulfil a certain task as it is fixed in the employment contract. Rather it is the obligation to the state as institution, independent of the individual task and independent of the political system.

As it had been said before on the typical *Beamte* is unique to the German system, going back in particular to *Lorenz von Stein* and his reform of the system of the public sector services. However, a strong parallel can be found particularly in Austria due to the historically strong link between the two states. There is an original own Austrian root as well, connected with the *Maria Theresian* order of the office *(Kanzleiordnung).* What is important as well is the fact that in most of the European countries in one way or another some characteristics can be fond which are very similar to the German *Beamte* and that in any case the official, employed by the statutory system has certain privileges and a higher degree of material but as well legal protection, linked to specific obligations.

To some extent elements, that had been originally characteristic for the *Beamtentum* had been transferred (a) on other employees in the public sector and (b) on employees working in agencies acting on behalf of the state, as e.g. not least employees in welfare organisations. This concerns some legal and material privileges but more importantly the commitment to loyalty, in particular in church organisations.

Even if we are concerned with typical German traditions we have to acknowledge at the same time that similar patterns can be found in many other countries. Again, it is commitment of loyalty that is for many times condition for taking up a position in a statutory service. Of particular interest is the resonance in the EU-law. Accordingly, the execution of some activities is reserved for nationals – in particular services in the security forces and police are concerned. Further, even if in a rather different way those professions that are covered by the regulation on the mutual recognition of diplomas (⇒ free movement) should be considered in this context alike.

A further remark has to be made: The strong position of the *Beamtentum,* the system of specific employment regulations in the public sector is since some years more and more under threat. Critiques see it as a matter that is not appropriate for modern societies.

D: Eine kurze Bemerkung zum Beamtentum ist erforderlich, insofern es sich dabei um die Stellung einer Gruppe von Beschäftigten handelt, die (a) typischerweise mit einem Großteil von Aufgaben im Sozialbereich befasst ist und (b) eine einmalige Stellung hat im deutschen System. Die Besonderheit ist dabei durch folgende Merkmale geprägt:

Unkündbarkeit

Merkmale der Versorgung wie Vergünstigungen bei

der Versteuerung, der Zahlung von Sozialabgaben ein besonderes Treueverhältnis gegenüber dem öffentlichen Arbeitgeber

Begründet ist dies System in der Loyalitätspflicht des Beamten. Diese Verpflichtung geht über die in einem Arbeitsvertrag geregelten Verpflichtungen hinaus und bezieht sich ferner auf den Staat, unabhängig vom jeweils gegebenen politischen System.

Wichtig ist ferner, dass ein Großteil der bestehenden Besonderheiten mit der Zeit auf verschiedene Bereiche übertragen wurde, in denen Aufgaben als gleichsam statuarische von beauftragten Organisationen und Institutionen erfüllt werden. Auch wenn dies nicht unbedingt in striktem Sinne gilt und auch wenn dies in unterschiedlichen Organisationen verschieden gehandhabt wird, so sind doch wichtige Elemente zumindest als Anklang zu finden. Zu nennen ist die Geltung des Tarifvertrages des öffentlichen Dienstes für Beschäftigte in Wohlfahrtsorganisationen. Auch wenn dieser Tarifvertrag zu unterscheiden ist von der Beamtenbesoldung, so zeigt sich doch zugleich die große Nähe zum staatlichen System. Ein anderer Aspekt ist die Loyalitätspflicht – so ist gerade in kirchlichen Wohlfahrtsorganisationen die Verpflichtung auf die Grundsätze der jeweiligen Glaubensgemeinschaft zu finden – und das kann eben durchaus bedeuten: die Erwartung einer "aktiven Zugehörigkeit" zur jeweiligen Religionsgemeinschaft.

Auch wenn es sich ganz wesentlich um eine spezifisch deutsche Tradition handelt, so ist doch zugleich darauf hinzuweisen, dass auch in anderen Ländern einige Merkmale durchaus ähnlich sind. Und wiederum ist es die besondere Treuepflicht, die oftmals eine Bedingung für die Annahme im Staatsdienst ist. Von besonderer Bedeutung ist hier nicht zuletzt auch der Niederschlag im EU-Recht. Hiernach ist die Beschäftigung in bestimmten Berufen auf jeweilige Staatsangehörige beschränkt. Dies betrifft vor allem "sicherheitssensible" Tätigkeiten (wie im Militär, den inneren Sicherheitskräften). Interessant sind hier – wenn auch völlig anders gelagert – Professionen aus Bereichen, die unter die Regelungen der gegenseitigen Anerkennung von Diplomen fallen (⇒ Freizügigkeit, auch: öffentliche Dienste).

Bewusstmachung

Verschiedene Begriffe scheinen zumindest sehr Ähnliches zu meinen. Zu unterscheiden sind aber zumindest die folgenden Dimensionen:

die individuell-psychologische Dimension;

diejenige der Weckung eines allgemein gesellschaftlich-sozialen Bewusstseins,

jene der Politisierung, also eines spezifischen gesellschaftlich-sozialen Bewusstseins

die praktische Dimension der Bewusstmachung und Politisierung.

Case Work

⇒ social intervention

Charity

In the common use this term corresponds best with the German term ⇒ *Wohlfahrtsverband,* even if the latter is better translated as welfare association. Most likely the reason is that the first impression of the term charity reminds the German speaker of the traditional concept of caritas, i.e. "love of the needy other as it is motivated by the Christian faith" (hence Caritas as name of the catholic welfare association). However, the charity is based on a secular concept and includes not least financial advantages as the charitable status, i.e. *Gemeinnützigkeit.*

Citizenship of the European Union

The citizenship of the European Union had been introduced into the European primary law with the Treaty of Maastricht. It does not replace the national citizenship; it consists of a variety of individual rights and duties as they are defined in the Treaty. In particular it refers to the following general additional rights:

freedom to move and right of residence in any of the member states of the EU;

right of active and passive vote in the country of residence for local and European elections;

diplomatic and consular protection outside of the EU by any of the national authorities of the member states where the member state of which the person in question is a national is not represented;

right of petition and appeal to the European Ombudsman.

⇒ Shengen agreement

Citizenship

In general, the concept of citizenship is caught between the two dimensions of (a) a belonging to a community, based on general rights and duties and (b) a limited understanding, being based on the belonging to a nation state. It is in particular during the last years that we can find a shift of the understanding into the direction of the more general understanding. This is not least to be seen in connection with processes of the dissolution of the nation state. Processes of migration on the one hand, international integration on the other hand play a role in this regard. What can be found in consequence can be called a problematisation of the nation state in general with two different, to some extent contradicting patterns. The one is the reflection on more fundamental questions of rights and obligations, connected with the search for what finally defines a community and the belonging to the community. The renaissance of *T.M. Marshall's* book Citizenship and Social Class *(in: Marshall, Tom H./Tom Bottomore: Citizenship and Social Class; London - Concord, Mass. 1992: 1 ff.)* is surely an expression of this. The other trend is that with the crisis of the legitimacy of the conventional state a revival of small communities can be found. Nationalism and regionalism are "lived concepts" and as such of relevance here. In any case, the meaning of nation, nationality and citizenship by naturalisation are gaining a new meaning in this context and have to be rethought.

⇒ citizenship of the EU; ⇒ Shengen

Civil Society

Quite a confusion is linked to the term civil society. Originally it had been used as a positive term, i.e. defined by its own characteristics. It had been in particular *Alexis de Toqueville* who first conceptualised civil society as a distinct and important element of the social order, connecting it to the idea of civic virtues – rights and obligations alike. What had been clear already from his understanding was a certain distinction or even confrontation of the state and the civil society. Although, the conceptualisation of civil society had been closely linked to the emergence of the nation state as we know it today *Toqueville* conceptualised civil society very much as complementing and even backing the state, thus it was being closely linked to the concept of mediation between the individual and the state. Note: The concept of mediation is again closely linked to the structure of medieval societies.

Later, civil society had been re-introduced into social science by *Antonio Gramsci*. In his understanding civil society was, however, distinct not just in terms of a distinct element of a nevertheless homogenous structure. Rather, his view on the civil society was more led by the idea of a distinct social space that stands in some way against the state, being at the same time colonialised by it and nevertheless a space to develop powers against the state in its given form.

Though these two classical positions are more or less clearly defined they had been point of departure for a confusing debate that changed the focus from the positively defined civil society to a negative definition, i.e. a definition that did not come from the generic elements of civil society itself. Instead, civil society had been seen as compounded social "sector", consisting of "non-entities". This was basically located "between" the market and the state, in some views between the market, the state and the private/family. As such it was seen as being non-profit-organisations/not-for-profit-organisations, non-governmental organisations etc., all basically not defined by what they are but more by what thgey are not.

From here it is not only that we see the loss of "generic" characteristics as the civic virtue emphasised by e.g. *Tocqueville.* In addition it is from here that issues as the tension between professional/voluntary work, the formal and informal et altera arise. What has to be emphasised is that this terminological shift, in fact, is a change in reality, i.e. the change of the role and position of civil society in the developed western societies.

CLIENT

"The client ('cluens', one who obeys) was a freedman, a captive, or one who attached himself to a patron ('jus applicationis'). He bore the same 'nomen gentilicium' as his patron, worshipped with him, and was indebted to him for 'obsequium, opere, bona,' respect, services, property … In return, his patron, under penalty of being devoted to the infernal gods ('Sacer esto'), gave him protection before the courts and outside of them, treated him with justice in the family circle, and gave him assistance in case of need." *(Brissaud, Jean: A History of French Public Law; London 1915: 12 f.)*

CO-DECISION PROCEDURE

⇒ Law

COMMUNICATION

⇒ Law

COMMUNITISATION

Transfer of matters which are dealt with on an ⇒ intergovernmental basis as laid down in the second or third pillar to the community method of the first pillar (⇒ Community law).

Probably the most important example is the communitisation of the free movement which, had been originally dealt with as part of the tasks of the cooperation on justice and home affairs under the third pillar and which is subsequently communitised, i.e. brought under the first pillar.

Community Acquis

Existing legal provisions which add up to the primary and secondary law of the European institutional system. The appreciation of the acquis is the fundamental precondition of the member status.

Community Initiative

Part of the work in the framework of the ESF which is carried out as being immediately a matter of the European Level. Even if in any case the ESF and the work in project frameworks is highly furnished there is a clear limitation: The evaluation is more or less oriented on a short-term basis. So, the crucial problem is how to transfer the praxis that can be found under these exceptional conditions into day-to-day practice.

Community law

The legal system of the European Communities is not only subdivided into different types of legal provisions (⇒ law). Rather, another differentiation refers to what is commonly known as the different pillars. These reflect the different pillars and mainly the difference between the European Union and the European Communities. We find three pillars, each concerned with a specific substantial area, different in their status depending on the degree of common responsibility and mutual coordination. These pillars are concerned with

"* the Community dimension, comprising the arrangements set out in the ESC, ECSC and Euratom Treaties, i.e. Union citizenship, Community policies, economic and monetary union etc. (first pillar);
* the common foreign and security policy, which comes under the Title V of the EU Treaty (second pillar);
* police and judicial cooperation in criminal matters, which comes under Title VI of the EU Treaty (third pillar)."

The division is not final (⇒ Communitisation).

Community work

⇒ Social intervention

Community

Community is best understood as a process of living together that develops and at the same time relies on common interests. As such, communities can be based on spatial processes or/and coherence which is built around "issues". In other words, it is build on identity or a sense of belonging. It is argued that community depends upon a collective imagining of difference or similarity. Sociology's relationship with the concept of community has been ambivalent as the decline of community has been predicted in many quarters.

Core aspects of communities are built around power, responsibility, and control. Of these the latter two are directed internally, i.e. aiming on control over and responsibility for the own life. Power is in this context – even if as well concerned with power balanced with the power of others – very much an issue of control over the own life of the community. For this reason, community has become an important site of social intervention and a central target of anti-poverty work or strategies. For this, cohesion is an important part of community building.

What is interesting is the obvious readiness of accepting the meaning and even importance of communities on the one hand and the hesitation in acknowledging them in real terms, i.e. beyond a "symbolic policy". The ambivalence is shown for example in the contradicting character of the policies in this area as they are envisaged by the European Commission. In fact we can speak of the establishment of limited points for access.

Note: Community is not (necessarily) concerned with non-hierarchical, democratic relationships.

Context

⇒ environment

Convergence criteria

To ensure that the sustainable convergence required for the achievement of economic and monetary union (EMU) comes about, the Treaty sets five convergence criteria which must be met by each Member State before it can take part in the third stage of EMU. The Commission and the European Central Bank (ECB) draw up reports to check whether the criteria are being met. The criteria are:

* the ratio of government deficit to gross domestic product must not exceed 3%;
* the ratio of government debt to gross domestic product must not exceed 60%;
* there must be a sustainable degree of price stability and an average inflation rate, observed over a period of one year before the examination, which does not exceed by more than one and a half percentage points that of the three best performing Member States in terms of price stability;
* there must be a long-term nominal interest rate which does not exceed by more than two percentage points that of the three best performing Member States in terms of price stability;
* the normal fluctuation margins provided for by the exchange-rate mechanism on the European Monetary system must have been respected without severe tensions for at least the last two years before the examination.

The convergence criteria, then, are meant to ensure that economic development within EMU is balanced and does not give rise to any tensions between the Member States. It must also be remembered that the criteria relating to government deficit and government debt must continue to be met after the start of the third stage of EMU (1 January 1999). A stability pact with this end in view was adopted at the Amsterdam European Council in June 1997. (glossary, Internet-version)

CO-ORDINATION, OPEN METHOD OF ⇒ Law

COREPER – COMMITTEE DE REPRESENTATIVES PERMANENTES

Coreper, the French acronym by which the Permanent Representatives Committee is known, consists of the Member States' Permanent Representatives (Ambassadors) and is responsible, at a stage involving preliminary negotiations, for assisting the Council of the European Union in dealing with the items on its agenda (proposals and drafts of instruments put forward by the Commission). It occupies a pivotal position in the Community decision-making system, in which it is at one and the same time a forum for dialogue (among the Permanent Representatives and between them and their respective national capitals) and a body which exercises political control (by laying down guidelines for, and supervising, the work of the expert groups). It is in fact divided in two to enable it to deal with all the tasks it has to carry out:

Coreper I, consisting of the Deputy Permanent Representatives, and

Coreper II, consisting of the Permanent Representatives themselves. (glossary, Internet version)

DASEINSVORSORGE

Der Begriff ist wohl ein deutsches Unikum. Eingeführt in die politische und rechtliche Wissenschaft und Diskussion wurde er von *Ernst Forsthoff (Die Verwaltung als Leistungsträger; Stuttgart/Berlin: Kohlhammer, 1938).* Der Bezug *Forsthoff's* war zunächst allgemein-soziologischer Art und bestimmte sich aus dem Allgemeininteresse. Weder konkretisierte *Forsthoff* dieses Allgemeininteresse noch arbeitete er heraus, wer denn die Definition bestimmen sollte.

Grundsätzlich sind in der allgemeinen Form jene Leistungen gemeint, die für die Sicherung der menschlichen Existenz notwendig sind. Ein wichtiger Bezugspunkt war gegeben mit dem Bezug auf den Staat als Produzenten/Erbringer und Regler. "Während der Mensch in vorindustriellen Zeiten noch einen unmittelbaren Zugang zu den Gütern hatte, die er zum Leben braucht, könne er sich selber diesen Zugang nun nicht mehr sichern – und der Verwaltung falle die Aufgabe zu, jedem die Möglichkeit zu eröffnen, an die benötigten Lebensgüter zu kommen. Daseinsvorsorge konzentriert sich danach nach *Forsthoff* auf „die Darbringung von Leistungen, auf welche der in die modernen massentümlichen Lebensformen verwiesene Mensch lebensnotwendig angewiesen ist' *(Forsthoff 1938, 7)." (Wolf Rainer Wendt: Wohlfahrt bewirtschaften ist mehr als öffentliche Daseinsvorsorge; in: Herrmann: Services of General Interests and Competition in Europe – touchstones for the social economy [Arbeitstitel]; Baden-Baden: Nomos, i.V.)*

Wenngleich die Definition des allgemeinen Interesses bei *Forsthoff* nicht zu finden ist, so wird doch aus dem soeben Zitierten zweierlei deutlich:

Das Allgemeininteresse ist eng auf die Existenzsicherung bezogen und in diesem Sinn zunächst nicht gesellschaftlich definiert; es ist aber sodann an die jeweils gegebenen Lebensformen geknüpft – somit wird das für die Existenzsicherung Erforderliche historisiert und damit im zweiten Schritt doch gesellschaftlich definiert.

Für die gegenwärtige Diskussion sind dabei vor allem folgende Differenzierungen von erheblicher – theoretischer und praktischer – Bedeutung. a) die Diskussion der Abgrenzung der Daseinsvorsorge gegenüber der Orientierung auf das generelle Interesse und b) die Diskussion des Zusammenhangs der Daseinsvorsorge mit einigen Begriffen, die gerne im Zusammenhang genannt werden, aber zumeist mehr oder weniger als Synonyme eingesetzt werden. Es handelt sich hier insbesondere um

* Gemeinwohlorientierte Leistungen
* Öffentliche Dienste
* Dienstleistungen von allgemeinem wirtschaftlichem Interesse
* Univeraldienst

Daseinsvorsorge scheint konzeptionell eindeutig festgelegt zu sein auf das zum Leben Erforderliche. Wenngleich dies im *Forsthoff'schen* Verständnis nicht auf das Existenzminimum sich bezieht, so ist es doch ein relativ eng umgrenzter Raum historisch-moralisch festgelegter Tatbestände. Der Begriff der Dienste des generellen Interesses bezieht sich der Verwendung nach auf den übergreifenden Charakter, d.h. jenen Tatbestand, dass ihr Nutzen der Bevölkerung insgesamt zu Gute kommt. Dies kann direkt erfolgen (⇒ Gemeinwohlorientierte Leistungen, dort die nichtwirtschaftlichen Tätigkeiten) oder aber indirekt durch die Wirtschaftsförderung in einer Region, deren Ergebnisse dann allgemein vorteilhaft sein sollten (⇒ Dienstleistungen von allgemeinem wirtschaftlichen Interesse).

Grundsätzlich lassen sich drei Muster unterscheiden, gegen deren Hintergrund die Daseinsvorsorge-Leistungen einzuordnen sind, namentlich

(1) ein stark staatlich und zentralistisch gestaltetes System, in dem ein hohes Maß an zentraler Kontrolle auch dann noch für bestimmte Dienste ausgeübt wird, wenn entsprechende Unternehmen privatisiert sind – Frankreich ist hier ein Musterbeispiel;

(2) ein stark privat orientiertes System, wie es mittlerweile in England besteht und in dem der private Charakter hervorgehoben wird – staatliche Kontrolle begrenzt sich hier stark auf einen administrativen Prozess;

(3) ein hybrides System, in dem eine Vielfalt von Eigentumsformen einhergeht mit einer Vielfalt und teils Undurchschaubarkeit von Kontrollmechanismen.

Für Frankreich kann übrigens festgestellt werden, dass es sehr verschiedene Organisationsformen hat – als Beispiele könnten genannt werden die Tätigkeiten im Bereich der *Économie plurielle* oder auch die *Services supplémentaires.*

DASEINSVORSORGE, *DIENSTLEISTUNGEN VON ALLGEMEINEM INTERESSE* – AUSNAHMEN DER GELTUNG DES WETTBEWERBSRECHTS

Es muss sich um nichtwirtschaftliche Aktivitäten handeln, wobei die Definition teils auf EU-Ebene erfolgen kann ('generische Bereiche') oder aber auf der nationalen Ebene, wobei der Umverteilungsaspekt eine wichtige Rolle spielt.

Es darf kein 'Handel' betroffen sein.

Eine *de minimis* Klausel ist eingesetzt, nach der die Tätigkeit ihrer Größe wegen als nicht bedeutsam definiert sein kann.

Vorgesehen ist eine 'ausnahmsweise Zulässigkeit', die sich nach *Artikel 78* und *87 (3)* respektive des *Vertrages von Amsterdam* wie folgt definiert: Es handelt sich um "Beihilfen, die den Erfordernissen der Koordinierung des Verkehrs oder der Abgeltung bestimmter, mit dem Begriff des öffentlichen Dienstes zusammenhängender Leistungen entsprechen" oder "zur Förderung von Kultur und der Erhaltung des kulturellen Erbes" dienen (e.g.: Beihilfen für Kleinbetriebe; Unterstützung für Problemgebiete; Beschäftigungsprogramme; Qualifizierungsprogramme; Regionalpolitik; Umweltschutz; F&E).

Ein weiterer Ausnahmebereich besteht in Unternehmen, die von der öffentlichen Hand mit ⇒ Dienstleistungen von allgemeinem wirtschaftlichen Interesse betraut sind *(s. Kommissionsmitteilung zur Daseinsvorsorge; COM 2000-580).*

Weiterhin von grundsätzlicher Bedeutung sind die Prüfkriterien, bei denen wiederum drei Aspekte genannt werden müssen, namentlich

* Neutralität gegenüber dem Eigentum
* Gestaltungsfreiheit bei der nationalen Definition sowie
* Wahrung der Verhältnismäßigkeit.

DIENSTLEISTUNGEN VON ALLGEMEINEM WIRTSCHAFTLICHEM INTERESSE

Ebenfalls auf das Interesse der Allgemeinheit bezogen,

finden sich auch hier besondere Gemeinwohlverpflichtungen (s.a. ⇒ Gemeinwohlorientierte Leistungen). Die Besonderheit besteht allerdings darin, dass die Leistungen hier strikt auf den Markt bezogen sind, d.h. sie gleichsam auf die Sicherung der Infrastruktur zielen. *Artikel 16* des *Amsterdamer Vertragswerkes* spezifiziert das Verständnis, indem diesen Leistungen eine besondere Funktion hinsichtlich der territorialen und sozialen Kohäsion zugeschrieben wird.

DIPLOME, GEGENSEITIGE ANERKENNUNG VON ~N

⇒ Freizügigkeit

DIRECTIVE

⇒ law

DISABILITY

Even if frequently used the term is "politically incorrect". It should read "people with special needs". The new term is in general accepted and used. However, the concept behind it is still lacking sufficient recognition. Furthermore (and reflecting the lack of recognition) in cases of "applied use" (e.g. disability allowance) it is nearly impossible yet to expect such a politically correct use.

Another aspect is that it is possible to distinguish a more critical usage of the term where *disability* is seen to be socially constructed and reinforced. In this usage it is not an individual's physical, psychological or educational status that is seen to be 'disabling' but instead it is society's inability to embrace difference and to equalise access and participation that are understood as problematic. However, it is important to see such debate more as an expert approach that does up to now not translate into a public debate and the public politically incorrect use of the term disability.

EEIG

European Economic Interest Grouping. Instrument to make transnational cooperation possible. The EEIG does not focus on the third partners. Instead, the objective is to look after the members own interest. It had been suggested to be a means to overcome the difficulties of the lack of a European or international legal status for private, non-profit organisations.

Empowerment

Empowerment hat mittlerweile wohl im Sozialbereich einen internationalen Platz erhalten und wird nicht mehr übersetzt. Wichtig ist aber, den Hintergrund zu beachten. Die Verbreitung des Begriffs geht vor allem auf gemeinwesenorientierte Arbeit im sozialen und politischen Bereich der so genannten Dritte-Welt-Länder zurück. Damit ist zugleich – auch im Falle der Übertragung des Begriffs in den Europäischen Sprachraum – eine inhaltliche Vorgabe gemacht. Es geht um eine "Befähigung" von Menschen für aktives und gesellschaftsveränderndes Handeln. Zwar erlaubt dies die Offenheit des Konzeptes, erfordert diese gar. Aber zugleich ist eben die Richtung des erwarteten Prozesses strukturell vorgegeben. So muss darauf hingewiesen werden, dass eine Verwendung des Begriffes im anderen Zusammenhang – z.B. im Bereich der Sozialarbeit, insbesondere im Zusammenhang individuell orientierter Ansätze – problematisch ist. Hier ist eher von Befähigung = *enabling* zu sprechen.

ENVIRONMENT

While usually employed by the meaning of the natural surrounding and its meaning as natural resource to be exploited by mankind (and for that to be treated with care).

"The aim of Community environment policy is to preserve, protect and improve the quality of the environment and to protect people's health. It also sets great store by the prudent and rational use of natural resources. Lastly, it seeks to promote measures at international level to deal with regional or worldwide environmental problems (Article 174, formerly Article 130r)." (glossary, Internet version)

However, it has to be seen, and in fact, it is more and

more recognised, that environment includes as well the cultural context and the social dimension. As such it is self-referential.

In terminological regard it is important that *environment* is different from context. While the *environment* is basically seen as distinct, but at the same time immediately connected, i.e. "part of the system" the *context* is more detached. As such it is a point of reference, but not more. Even further detached is the *surrounding.*

EQUAL OPPORTUNITIES

The EU-glossary (Internet version) refers twice to this matter, the first time in general terms. Here it states:

"Two key elements of the general principle of equal opportunities are the ban on discrimination on grounds of nationality (Article 12 of the EC Treaty, formerly Article 6) and equal pay for men and women (Article 141 of the EC Treaty, formerly Article 119). It is intended to apply to all fields, particularly economic, social, cultural and family life.

The Treaty of Amsterdam added a new Article 13 to the Treaty, reinforcing the principle of non-discrimination, which is closely linked to equal opportunities. Under this new Article, the Council has the power to take appropriate action to combat discrimination based on sex, racial or ethnic origin, religion or belief, disability, age or sexual orientation."

The second mention is concerned with equal treatment for men and women and here the glossary states:

"As early as 1957, Article 141 (former Article 119) of the EC Treaty laid down the principle that men and women should receive equal pay for equal work. Since 1975 a series of directives have broadened the principle to cover access to employment, training and career progression and working conditions, the aim being to eliminate all forms of discrimination at work. Equal treatment was later extended to social security, statutory schemes and occupational schemes. In the 1980s recognition of this principle led to the promotion of equal opportunities via multiannual programmes.

The Treaty of Amsterdam seeks to supplement Article 141 (which is rather limited in scope, covering only equal pay) by including the promotion of equality between men and women as one of the tasks of the Community set out in Article 2 of the EC Treaty."

For many times it remains unclear in the official jargon if and how equal treatment and equal opportunities are linked. Furthermore and more fundamentally: the structural patterns of what can be called a patriarchal society are basically neglected. Thus, equality measures do have very much of a "compensating" character, providing "supplementing" services and/or means.

Terminological confusion arise time and again when terms as equal opportunities, equal rights, equal treatment are not distinguished in there very specific meaning.

EUROBAROMETER

Surveys undertaken regularly to explore the public opinion in particular on the process of European Integration and its public perception. In parallel a study is undertaken investigating key policy maker's opinion. Furthermore, surveys on specific topics are carried out (varied as for instance European's and holidays or Racist attitudes).

FOKUSGRUPPE

Fokusgruppen versammeln Personen, die hinsichtlich einer ganz bestimmten Problemlage besonders fachkundig sind. Dabei kann die Expertise auch unter Umständen in der herausragenden Kenntnis eines Gebietes, etwa eines Stadtteils bestehen. Die Rolle ist nicht zuletzt in der Vermittlung verschiedener Interessen zu sehen. Anders verhält es sich bei den Ressourcengruppen, die eher den Charakter eines Mobilisierungspotentials aufweisen. Zwar besteht auch hier eine besondere Art des Expertentums, allerdings ist dies mehr mit der Ausnutzung des Bestehenden als mit der Entwicklung von Neuem verbunden. In diesem Zusammenhang sind auch *Schlüsselpersonen* zu erwähnen. Hierbei handelt es sich um Personen, die aufgrund welcher Eigenschaften auch immer eine Vermittlungsposition beziehen. Eine solche Position kann auf guten Verbindungen, guter Kenntnis der Umstände, Macht, Ressourcen oder anderem beruhen.

FREE MOVEMENT OF PERSONS (VISAS, ASYLUM, IMMIGRATION AND POLICIES)

⇒ Freizügigkeit

FREIZÜGIGKEIT

Es handelt sich um eine der Vier Grundfreiheiten – was sich hier auf Personen bezieht, bezieht sich bei den anderen drei Freiheiten auf das Kapital, die Waren und die Dienstleistungen. Gerade die letztgenannte Freiheit macht deutlich, dass insbesondere Berufstätigkeiten im Sozialbereich aber nicht schlicht eine Frage der Freizügigkeit der Person sind, sondern auch in enger Verbindung mit der Freizügigkeit der entsprechenden Arbeitgeber verbunden ist. Letzteres ist insbesondere auch eine Frage der Dienste der ⇒ Daseinsvorsorge, der ⇒ Dienstleistungen von allgemeinem wirtschaftlichem Interesse bzw. der ⇒ Gemeinwohlorientierten Leistungen. Gerade was die Trägerstrukturen in diesem Bereich anbelangt, herrscht derzeit einige Verwirrung. Durch die Vorlage einer Mitteilung der Kommission unter dem Titel "Leistungen der Daseinsvorsorge" *(Brüssel, 20.9.2000; KPM 2000_580 endg.)* fühlen sich insbesondere die deutschen Träger der Freien Wohlfahrtspflege bedroht. Aber auch über diese Interessengruppe hinaus sind zweifellos Änderungen im Bereich der Erbringung von Sozialdiensten zu erwarten.

Allgemein wird EU-offiziell zur Freizügigkeit festgestellt:

"Mit dem Amsterdamer Vertrag wurde in den EG-Vertrag ein neuer Titel IV für folgende Materien aufgenommen:

* Freizügigkeit

* Kontrollen an den Außengrenzen
* Asyl, Einwanderung und Schutz der Rechte von Angehörigen dritter Länder
* justitielle Zusammenarbeit in Zivilsachen

Diese Bereiche waren zuvor Titel VI des EU-Vertrags (Justiz und Inneres) zugeordnet. Mit dem Amsterdamer Vertrag sind sie "vergemeinschaftet", d.h. in den Rechtsrahmen des ersten Pfeilers einbezogen worden. Praktisch wird diese Veränderung allerdings nur schrittweise im Laufe von fünf Jahren nach Inkrafttreten des neuen Vertrags vollzogen.

Nach diesem Übergangszeitraum wird der Rat in diesen Bereichen nicht mehr allein tätig, sondern auf Vorschlag der Kommission entscheiden. Außerdem werden auf absehbare Zeit die Mitentscheidung und die Abstimmung mit qualifizierter Mehrheit zur Anwendung kommen. Schließlich ist der Gerichtshof nunmehr für Auslegungsfragen im Zusammenhang mit den Materien dieses neuen Titels IV zuständig.

Das Vereinigte Königreich und Irland werden sich nicht an den im Rahmen des Titels IV erlassenen Maßnahmen beteiligen. Dänemark wird sich nur an den Maßnahmen betreffend die Visaerteilung beteiligen." *(EU-Glossar, Internet-Version)*

Von besonderer Bedeutung ist vor allem für Professionelle, die die diese Freizügigkeit in die Tat umsetzen wollen, die grundsätzliche Anerkennung der Diplome. Diplome, die in einem Mitgliedsland der EU erworben sind, werden hiernach auch in den anderen Ländern anerkannt. Dies ist vor allem für die Sozialberufe von großer Bedeutung, als es z.B. SozialarbeiterInnen, Mitgliedern der Pflegeprofession, Professionellen aus dem Erziehungsbereich und anderen Berufen die Aufnahme einer Berufstätigkeit in einem anderen Land erheblich erleichtert. Die Regelungen finden sich – vor allem – in der Richtlinie 89/48/EWG des Rates vom 21. Dezember 1988 über eine allgemeine Regelung zur Anerkennung der Hochschuldiplome, die eine mindestens dreijährige Berufsausbildung abschließen (*Amtsblatt nr. L 019 vom 24/01/1989 S. 0016 – 0023)*. “Vor allem“ bedeutet, dass daneben Bestimmungen besonderer Art bestehen, teils mit besonderen Regelungen für einige Berufe verbunden. Etwas vereinfacht lässt sich feststellen, dass

* grundsätzlich die Anerkennung für bestimmte Berufe und Berufsgruppen getroffen wurde;
* je nach Professionsbereich und Land entweder eine Zusatzprüfung abgelegt werden muss oder aber eine Einführungszeit abzuleisten ist – der Sinn dessen besteht darin, zumindest die generelle Eingewöhnung und vor allem auch die Kenntnis von “ortsüblichen Besonderheiten“ zu ermöglichen;
* zuständig für die konkreten Regelungen und die Überprüfung ihrer Einhaltung in den meisten Fällen die jeweiligen Ministerien für Erziehung sind, bei denen sich Kontaktpersonen befinden, teils aber auch Wirtschaftsministerien oder besondere Agenturen, die mit Fragen der akademischen Berufe befasst sind.

GEMEINDEENTWICKLUNG

⇒ Gemeindeplanung

GEMEINDEPLANUNG

Abzugrenzen von der Gemeindeentwicklung, wobei die Gemeindeentwicklung durchaus Teil der Gemeindeplanung sein kann und sein sollte. Die Gemeindeentwicklung zielt auch auf die (subjektive und handlungsmäßige) Dimension der Potenziale der Gemeinde und schlägt sich nicht unbedingt in einer Infrastruktur nieder (sie hat diese freilich zur Voraussetzung und zeitigt sie teils Konsequenz; ist aber hiervon unabhängig). Gemeindeplanung, oft ebenso prozesshaft, zielt aber eindeutig im Ergebnis auf eine Änderung der Umwelt, ist sekundär eine Änderung der Menschen in der und durch die Umwelt. Teilweise – wenn auch nicht unbedingt bewusst – handelt es sich um das Wiederaufleben von Ansätzen, die im Rahmen der soziologischen Planungstheorien der 60er/70er Jahre bereits eine gewisse Hochkonjunktur hatten.

GEMEINWIRTSCHAFT

So eindeutig dieser Begriff auf den ersten Blick und dem Grunde nach ist, so ist doch auf einige Besonderheiten hinzuweisen. Grundsätzlich handelt es sich um 'halböffentliche' Unternehmen. Ursprünglich auf den makroökonomischen Bereich bezogen (ordnungspolitische Idee der Gemeinwirtschaft; s.a. ⇒ Sozialökonomie), liegt der Bezug heute eher auf der Unternehmensebene. Es finden sich sodann die folgenden Typen:

* öffentliche Unternehmen
* freigemeinwirtschaftliche Unternehmen, darunter Genossenschaften sowie widmungswirtschaftliche Unternehmen (nichtwirtschaftliche Deckung fremden Bedarfs)
* öffentlich gebundene Unternehmen.

Durch die unterschiedlichen Entwicklungen in den verschiedenen Ländern haben die jeweiligen Stränge der Gemeinwirtschaft eine sehr unterschiedliche Stellung im ökonomischen Gesamtsystem. Insbesondere in Frankreich und Italien finden sich solche Unternehmensformen stark verbreitet und sind vor allem auch für die örtliche und regionale Wirtschaftsentwicklung von großer Bedeutung. Auch heute noch hat dort der Selbsthilfecharakter eine große Relevanz, wenngleich in allen Ländern mittlerweile die Groß-Genossenschaften eine dominante Rolle spielen (oder spielten und mittlerweile den Gemeinwirtschaftscharakter völlig aufgegeben haben; s.a. ⇒ Sozialökonomie). Ein weiteres Charakteristikum insbesondere für Italien und Irland ist, dass die Kooperativen eine besondere Bedeutung in Bereichen einnehmen, die nach deutschem Verständnis eher durch politische Organisationen und/oder Sozialdienste abgedeckt würden.

Gemeinwohlorientierte Leistungen

Gemeinwohlorientierte Leistungen sind marktbezogene oder nicht marktbezogene Leistungen, die im Interesse der Allgemeinheit erbracht und daher von den Behörden mit spezifischen Gemeinwohlverpflichtungen verknüpft werden. Sie umfassen nichtwirtschaftliche Tätigkeiten (Pflichtschulwesen, soziale Sicherheit usw.), hoheitliche Aufgaben (Sicherheit, Justiz usw.) und Dienstleistungen von allgemeinem wirtschaftlichen Interesse (Energieversorgung, Kommunikation usw.). Artikel 86 (ex-Artikel 90) des EG-Vertrags findet nicht Anwendung auf die nichtwirtschaftlichen Tätigkeiten und die hoheitlichen Aufgaben.

General Interest Services

"General-interest services" are services considered to be in the general interest by the public authorities and accordingly subjected to specific public-service obligations. They include non-market services (e.g. compulsory education, social protection), obligations of the State (e.g. security and justice) and services of general economic interest (e.g. energy and communications). Article 86 of the Treaty (former Article 90) does not apply to the first two categories (non-market services and state obligations). (glossary, Internet version)

Gesetz

⇒ law

GROUP WORK

⇒ social intervention

Intergovernmental, international, supranational

When talking about current processes that take place beyond the nation state it is important to be aware of the fact that the term *international* is a term that encompasses three different relationships. International, as a heading term, has at the same time a specific meaning, relating to a variety of relationships between at least two nations. Actually, for relationships between two nations mostly the term *bilateral* is employed. However, bilateral is more concerned with the number of the sides than with the character of the relations. *Supranational* is concerned with matters that may arise from nation states. But the actual dealing with them in a *supranational* way does not reflect individual interests of the actors, rather, stemming from the nation, they are usually being treated in the perspective of the suggested common interest of the "community". *Intergovernmental* refers to the relations between governments, different compared to *international* – a term referring to the whole variety of possible actors. In the *intergovernmental* relationship we have to face the fact that the national interests are still the guiding principles.

Law

Rather than attempting to give a brief introduction into the wide range of legal provision we will point on some important terms of which the legal meaning will not be finally explained. Mainly we are concerned with following "instruments":

Contract: mainly agreement between individuals or individual institutions. "Private" arrangement, (e.g. contract of employment, contract of sale)

Treaty: mainly agreement or arrangement on the level of institutions, in particular "the state" or between states. Even if the term is used as well for "private" arrangements it is in our context in particular used for the arrangements between the member states to define the fundamental, constitutional-like regulations. This, then, is called as well the ***primary law.***

The ***secondary law*** is supplementing the primary law, clarifying what is formulated on a very general level in the primary provisions. Relevant are in particular:

recommendations, i.e. legally non-binding "suggestions" to communicate proposals for concrete measures from the Commission to the member States or other actors;

directives, i.e. instruments that require the Member

States to amend existing or introduce new national legislation to achieve the aims of the directive. It is, however, open to the member states by exactly which means these aims are approached;

regulations, these are the strongest form of Community legislation by which general rules are laid down. They are entirely binding and directly applicable in all Member States.

In addition ***communications*** by the Commission play an important role as means of information and with that they have an agenda-setting role.

So far, ***bills*** and ***acts*** had not been mentioned. Bills are basically meant as acts on the preparatory stage, drafts of acts. Acts, then, are laws as they had been adopted by the respective deciding body, on the national level mostly the Parliament. However, it is not clear and depending very much of the "local" use. Thus, it is unclear as well if a bill that has passed the Parliament, but is still not finally ratified by the head of state (President, Queen, King or whatever is appropriate in the country in question) is still considered as Bill or if it is already an Act.

Coming back to the European legal system and the legal instruments that are available for and in the EU-institutions some more aspects have to be considered even if they are not concerned with legal instruments in the strict sense.

`"The ***codecision procedure*** (Article 251 of the EC Treaty, formerly Article 189b) was introduced by the Treaty of Maastricht. It gives Parliament the power to adopt instruments jointly with the Council. In practice, it has strengthened Parliament's legislative powers in the following fields: the free movement of workers, right of establishment, services, the internal market, education (incentive measures), health (incentive measures), consumer policy, trans-European networks (guidelines), environment (general action programme), culture (incentive measures) and research (framework programme).” (EU-glossary, Internet version).

Besides this the ***co-operation procedure*** and the ***consultation procedure*** are of relevance in particular with view on the position of the European Parliament.

A recent development is the launch of the ***open method of co-ordination.*** This is meant as developing a closer link between the EU-bodies and other actors. Such a closer relationship is being implemented after the Lisbon summit in early 2000. The implicit aim is to practically define the principal of ⇒ subsidiarity as not just a question of alternative responsibilities in different areas. Rather, it is the attempt to develop a newer version of mutual support and completion.

MAINSTREAMING

(1) transformation of work, ideas approaches which had been developed and/or temporarily undertaken on a project basis. This may relate to projects, which had been limited in time or on a limited local/regional scale. Taking work out of such a limited frame and transforming them into mainstream work is understood as mainstreaming.

(2) Targeted work on a social-policy issue is taken out of the specialised, and as such limited application and translated into an issue on a higher level, i.e. its recognition and consideration is required in other, ideally all politics and policies.

Öffentliche Dienste

a) Einrichtung, die ein öffentlicher Dienst erbringt.

b) Leistung mit einem besonderen Gemeinwohlauftrag, der nicht zuletzt durch staatliche Auflagen erzwungen wird. Folgende zentralen Kriterien sollen nach der Charta der öffentlichen Dienste gelten:

* Versorgungskontinuität
* Qualität
* Versorgungssicherheit
* gleiche Zugangsmöglichkeiten
* ein erschwinglicher Preis
* soziale, kulturelle und ökologische Akzeptanz.

Open Method of Co-ordination ⇒ Law

Participation

Taking part *([lat.] pars capere)* – an important strategic aim of policy measures and programmes on EU level. The idea is (a) to find an effective mechanism of "translating policies into every days life", i.e. in this understanding to consequently apply the principle of subsidiarity in the process of policy development, decision making on the spot and implementation. (b) Emphasising participation is concerned with gaining a basis of legitimation for policy measures in particular and the European integration in general. It also means taking part or being involved in the development process. This is a highly contested term as participation is rarely universally realised and equally shared. What constitutes genuine participation and the means through which participation should be expressed are often controversial issues in community development and policy making alike.

Primary law

⇒ law

Recommendation

⇒ law

Regulation

⇒ law

Ressourcengruppen

⇒ Fokusgruppen

Risikostrukturausgleich

introduced 1992; system of balancing risk between health insurances in Germany.

Schlüsselpersonen

⇒ Fokusgruppen

Secondary law

⇒ LAW

Services of general economic interest

Services of general economic interest are commercial services of general economic utility, on which the public authorities therefore impose specific public-service obligations (Article 86 of the EC Treaty, formerly Article 90). Transport, energy and communications services are prime examples.

A new Article 16 has been written into the EC Treaty by the Treaty of Amsterdam, acknowledging the place occupied by services of general economic interest in the shared values of the Union and their role in promoting social and territorial cohesion. Article 16 also states that such services must operate on the basis of principles and conditions which enable them to fulfil their functions. (glossary, Internet version)

SHENGEN (AGREEMENT AND CONVENTION)

This agreement has been signed in June 1995 by Belgium, Germany, France, Luxembourg and the Netherlands. It is concerned with removing the "internal borders" and tightening the "external borders", i.e. all those borders to the so-called non-Shengen countries. The original Agreement was followed up in June 1990 by the Shengen Convention. Critical positions interpret this as a major step in finally defining a fortress Europe. Be it as it is the regulations have a major impact on Social Policy as they contribute to a strict definition of EU-citizens (⇒ citizenship). However, this statement has to be qualified. The *positive integration* by enhancing the status of the European citizen status is rather limited. There are no major changes for example in connection with the transfer of social benefits etc. However, what may be called *positive exclusion* is rather strict. It is strictly defined who falls under the Shengen aquis and who not.

SIGN LANGUAGE

Manual alphabets are distinct from signed languages. Singed languages as used by Deaf communities are indigenous naturally occurring languages with their own complex grammars. Of course, there are other invented sign languages, such as those used by enclosed orders and the sign languages of the plains indians. Further there are signed systems that have been created to present in a manual form, the structure of spoken languages. These were traditionally used in schools for the Deaf - but are not naturally occurring languages. They are systems that mark out the syntactic and morphological alterations of the spoken language in question. For example, signed English has a specific sign to mark for past tense -ed, a plural marker for nouns -s (which interestingly is used with plural nouns that do not take -s (e.g. mouse becomes mice, but in signed English, the signs MOUSE+S would be used.) Thus, absolute representation of the grammar system is not guaranteed. This contrasts with natural sign languages, like Irish Sign Language, where plurals are typically marked by repetition of the nominal (e.g. TREE TREE TREE - "trees" (or "forest") and where time is marked in a combination of ways, but not through tense marking on the verb, as is the case in English. Instead, aspectual modification, "timelines" and "specific time reference" are used to establish timeframes in most recorded sign languages.

Manual alphabets are another thing altogether; My colleague at the University of Bristol, Rachel Sutton-Spence, wrote her PhD thesis on the role of the manual alphabet and finger spelling in British Sign Language. She notes that "a manual alphabet is a series of hand arrangements corresponding to the letters of the alphabet. Manual alphabets are capable of representing any alphabet or syllabary. The British manual alphabet consists of 26 basic hand arrangements, corresponding to the 26 letters of the English alphabet. Each hand arrangement is a manual letter". Note however, that while the BSL manual alphabet is two-handed, all other European Sign Languages use one handed manual alphabets. "Finger spelling" entails spelling out words from the spoken languages using characters from the manual alphabet. Thus, each hand configuration represents a letter in a word. Nouns are the most frequently finger spelled items, typically people's names, names of streets, etc. Further, we find that finger spelling has influenced the form of sign languages insofar as some established signs use what are called "initialised handshapes" – the signs begin with, or include some form of handshape that comes from the manual alphabet – an example is the sign for kitchen which has a "k" handshape, produced by the signer's dominant hand in a circling movement a little lower than chest level.

SOCIAL ADMINISTRATION

⇒ Social intervention

SOCIAL INTERVENTION

There is a long debate, actually accompanying the whole history of social professions or even social science. Social science, in particular approaches employed by a humanist tradition, lead to the idea of the possibility of planning and "designing" human societies. Even if this general idea can be taken as momentum of consensus in modernising societies the ideas around how this can be achieved and implemented have been varied and often contradictory. Nevertheless, a field of approaches developed where the individual disciplines accepted despite all differences, a common ground and a fundamental feeling of affinity. Probably the most important disciplines had been – in our context and field of interest – social psychology, social pedagogy, social work, community work and social policy. Somewhat crosscutting is social administration, a strand that only recently emerged as a distinct discipline. However, as such it is more and more a detached area, solely employed by management issues (as such it is distinct from the German discuss on where *Sozialmanagement* claims to develop a very distinct pattern of management for the social sector.

The sequence, beginning with social psychology and going from there to social policy, is chosen to reflect somewhat the nearness and distance respectively to the individual and the societal level.

In any case, it has to be respected that this grouping is largely a "German-English" amalgam. The affinity to social psychology and social pedagogy and as well the inclusion of social administration is more owed to the German understanding – in England and Ireland they would not be considered as part of the affinity group – here named as social intervention. At the same time, to mention all the disciplines in one row follows more the English tradition. Even if social work and community work in particular are conflicting disciplines they are at least independent disciplines. Even if the claim for their scientific character is unclear the distinction remains in theory and practice. In Germany, on the other hand, *community work (Gemeinwesenarbeit)* basically would be understood as "method" of social work rather than to understand it in its independence, as having its own disciplinary rights.

The basic differences can probably seen in a comparison between the English, the French and the German tradition.

The German concept is a predominance of social work – a variety of approaches are basically subordinated and seen as methodology or just methods of this;

The English tradition suggests a rather strict, even competitive and contradictive distinction between the supposedly individualistic, curative strand of social work and the socially based and oriented, on change aiming community approach. Other areas are more or less methods, in part used in both areas (and as such courted);

The French concept can broadly be described as promoting a common roof for a variety of disciplines, each relatively independent. This allows as well the inclusion of a wider area of professional activities (including parts of care professions, which are mostly not seen as matter of interest) and the further differentiation and processes of getting

getting independent of newly emerging areas (⇒ Sozialarbeit).

Social pedagogy

⇒ Social intervention

Social Policy

⇒ Social intervention

Social Work

⇒ Social intervention

Soziale Arbeit

Im Gegensatz zum englischen Sprachbereich und Handlungsverständnis *(⇒ social intervention)* ist im deutschen Verständnis ein eher klares Verhältnis insofern gegeben, dass die Tradition einer klaren Hierarchie besteht. Soziale Arbeit bildet eine Art Oberbegriff und andere Bereiche werden nicht nur untergeordnet, sondern mehr noch als Methoden der Sozialarbeit gesehen. Der wohl auffälligste Bereich als Unterschied zum englischen Verständnis ist der Bereich der Gemeinwesenarbeit. In der Übersetzung würde man von *community work* sprechen. Zugleich muss dann aber festgestellt werden, dass *community work* ein eigenständiges Profil hat, gar in gewissem Gegensatz zur *social work* steht, wobei *social work* eben als strenge Übersetzung der Sozialarbeit steht. Solche Unterschiede sind von gravierender Bedeutung gerade auch im grenzüberschreitenden Bereich disziplinärer Diskussionen. Was besonders für Gemeinwesenarbeit – *community work* zutrifft, hat wohl ebenso seine Bedeutung für andere Bereiche, wie etwa das im französischen stark vertretene Konzept der *animation.* Was dort wiederum stark eigenständige disziplinäre Bedeutung hat, ist im Deutschen erstens wohl durch verschiedene Begriffe erfasst – z.B. Theaterpädagogik, Animation, Animationspädagogik. Wiederum handelt es sich dabei eher um Methoden der Sozialarbeit als um eigenständige Disziplinen. Was nun zugleich gesehen werden muss, sind folgende zwei Faktoren:

Das deutsche Verständnis der Sozialarbeit ist relativ

weit gefasst, weist mehr "Gesellschaftlichkeit" der Orientierung aus, als dies im englischsprachigen Bereich der Fall ist. In diesem Zusammenhang ist im Deutschen dann auch die Trennung zwischen Sozialarbeit und Sozialpädagogik zu sehen.

Zum anderen ist auch das deutsche Verständnis so eindeutig doch nicht, wie es dargestellt zu sein scheint. Offene Grenzen bestehen zunächst nicht zuletzt hinsichtlich eines wie auch immer zu fassenden Professionalitätsanspruchs. Angesprochen ist hier die Nähe, die zu ehrenamtlicher Arbeit, sozialer Bewegung, sozialen Aktionen auch im Sinn politischer Aktivitäten gesehen und akzeptiert bzw. abgelehnt wird. Auch dies wird verschiedentlich dann zu überbrücken versucht durch die Einführung einer Begriffsunterscheidung zwischen Sozialarbeit und Soziale Arbeit. In jedem Fall sind die Grenzen auch zu Sozialpolitik und – zumindest vor dem Hintergrund einer internationalen Perspektive – zu Bereichen von Pflegeberufen klar zu bestimmen.

Sozialkapital

Zwei Bedeutungen sind insbesondere zu unterscheiden. Einmal wird der Begriff verwendet, um besondere Fähigkeiten herauszuheben, die gleichsam als Einsatz auf dem Arbeitsmarkt oder bei der Suche und Ausnutzung besonderer Beziehungen eingesetzt werden können. Im Grunde folgt dies der Faktortheorie in der Ökonomie, geht über diese gar hinaus, als der "Nutzen" dieses Kapitals eben als allgemein von Bedeutung angesehen wird. Mit aller gebotener Vorsicht kann man von einer utilitaristischen Interpretation von Kontaktfreudigkeit sprechen. Aber: Hier wie auch im Folgenden handelt es sich (zumeist) nicht um ein strategisch eingesetztes Mittel.

Eine andere Verwendung sieht diesen Begriff im Licht einer kommunitaristischen Interpretation. Dann steht nicht die "Nutzbarmachung" im Vordergrund. Stattdessen geht es um allgemeine, nicht abrechenbare, nicht einmal strikt individuell zurechenbare “Leistungen“. Hier bedeutet der Begriff eher Geselligkeit, Solidarität, gegenseitige Verpflichtung und Abhängigkeit – je nach Perspektive, aber auch je nach der Haltung des Einzelnen oder der Gruppe (sei es der “Sozialkapitalbesitzer“ oder derjenigen, die in das Netz jener “Besitzer“ eingebunden [“gekauft“] werden).

SOZIALÖKONOMIE

Obgleich äußerst unscharf gefasst *(s. etwa Ulli Arnold/ Bernd Maelicke [Hrsg.]: Lehrbuch der Sozialwirtschaft; Baden-Baden: Nomos, 1998 – der Band zeigt eine Vielfalt der Begriffsverwendung),* so zeichnet sich doch im Gebrauch mehr und mehr eine abgeschwächte Variante der ordnungspolitischen Fassung der früheren ⇒ Gemeinwirtschaft ab. Die Besonderheit besteht darin, dass insbesondere auch Bereiche einbezogen sind, die in den 'zweiten Arbeitsmarkt', die 'Schattenwirtschaft' und prekäre Wirtschaftsorganisationen fallen.

Sozialstaat

The term *Sozialstaat* is not unique, nevertheless most common in German language. In other countries the aquivalent for the *Wohlfahrtsstaat* seems to be sufficient. The suggested difference between the social and the welfare state refers to a distinction between (a) a system of legal provisions, constituting the social state. On the other hand, however, the term welfare state is employed with a more general understanding of a general wellbeing of the population. Even if in both cases the state plays a fundamental role, such a difference can be made out as crucial in policy making. This gets in particular clear when we look at the Netherlands where the name of Ministries is borrowed from the aim rather than the target.

Of further importance in this context are the terms of the *social order,* being mainly concerned with the relationship of different groups on the macro-level and in particular its definition by the law;

political order, being employed by the political-institutional system as far as it is the basis for the relationship between the social groups;

social system, going beyond the legal and political perspective, covering the whole political and social culture.

Talking of different social groups refers, here, to the economic status and other criteria as for instance ethnical aspects alike.

SUBSIDIARITÄT:

D: Grundsatz der Verhältnismäßigkeit.

Das Europäische Primärrecht definiert folgendermaßen:

'Die Gemeinschaft wird innerhalb der Grenzen der ihr in diesem Vertrag zugewiesenen Befugnisse und gesetzten Ziele tätig.

In den Bereichen, die nicht in ihre ausschließliche Zuständigkeit fallen, wird die Gemeinschaft nach dem Subsidiaritätsprinzip nur tätig, sofern und soweit die Ziele der in Betracht gezogenen Maßnahmen auf Ebene der Mitgliedstaaten nicht ausreichend erreicht werden können und daher wegen ihres Umfangs oder ihrer Wirkungen besser auf Gemeinschaftsebene erreicht werden können.' *(Artikel 5 der konsolidierten Fassung des Vertrags zur Gründung der Europäischen Gemeinschaft – http://europa.eu.int/eur-lex/de/treaties/dat/ec_cons_treaty_de.pdf; 25.12.2001)*

Vergessen wird immer wieder, dass gleichsam komplementär die Grundsätze der Verhältnismäßigkeit und der Notwendigkeit zueinander stehen. Damit knüpfen sich an jede Gemeinschaftsaktion drei Fragen:

Erstens: Ist der anvisierte Aktionsbereich überhaupt EU-relevant, d.h. sind damit Bereiche betroffen, die für die Verwirklichung der Vertragsziele stehen?

Zweitens: Wenn dies prinzipiell der Fall ist, ist zu klären, ob wirklich ein Aktivwerden seitens der EU-Institutionen gefordert ist oder ob nicht die darunter liegenden Einheiten besser oder doch ebenso gut die Ziele erreichen können.

Drittens: Das Verhältnismäßigkeitsprinzip bezieht sich darauf, die Regelungsdichte und Regelungstiefe möglichst gering zu halten. M.a.W. selbst wenn EU-Aktionen als notwendig erachtet werden, sollen sie möglichst viel Raum für die unteren Ebenen lassen.

Damit ist neben das Subsidiaritätsprinzip dasjenige der Proportionalität auf gleiche Ebene gestellt.

Von besonderer Beachtung sollte eine Berücksichtigung der Besonderheiten des Verständnisses auf nationaler Ebene sein. Dabei gilt es, zwei Dimensionen zu beachten:

1) die 'Formalisierung' des Subsidiaritätsgrundsatzes. So ist beispielsweise die Superiorität der BAGFW-Verbände wohl in keinem anderen Lande in dieser Form zu finden. Eine andere Art von Superiorität findet sich in Spanien mit der Blindenorganisation ONCE, die gleichsam im Resultat zu einem ähnlichen Muster der Subsidiarität führt, aber von einer völlig anderen Seite, namentlich einem 'natürlichen Monopol' der Organisation her begründet ist Andererseits finden sich die gleichsam 'ungeregelten Zustände' in Irland, wo Subsidiarität 'im Rechtssinn nicht besteht, aber praktiziert wird'.

2) die Verbindung mit möglicherweise bestehenden Partnerschaftsvereinbarungen, i.e. korporatistischen Systemen. Die mittlerweile weitreichende Entwicklung des irischen Korporatismus mit der expliziten Einbeziehung von ⇒ Wohlfahrtsverbänden als eigene 'Säule' ist ein herausragendes Beispiel in diesem Zusammenhang.

E: Principle of the catholic Social Teaching, explicitly and pronouncedly formulated in the encyclica *Rerum Novarum* and encyclica *Quadragessimo Anno* It asserts that 'a community of a higher order should not interfere in the internal life of a community of a lower order, depriving the latter of its functions, but rather should support it in case of need and help to coordinate its activity with the activities of the rest of society'.

The *Article 3 b* of *Treaty of the European Union,* as decided upon in Amsterdam, reads:

'The Community shall act within the limits of the powers conferred upon it by this Treaty and of the objectives assigned to it therein.

In areas which do not fall within its exclusive competence, the Community shall take action, in accordance with the principle of subsidiarity, only if and in so far as the objectives of the proposed action cannot be sufficiently achieved by the Member States and can therefore, by reason of the scale or effects of the proposed action, be better achieved by the Community.

Any action by the Community shall not go beyond what is necessary to achieve the objectives of this Treaty.'

Thus, three basic questions have to be clarified, i.e.

First, if the matter of concern is relevant to put into place the aims and objectives of European integration as laid down in the Treaty

Second – and if this is the case – if it is necessary that actions have to be undertaken by the European institutions or if measures can be defined that can be implemented on the sub-European level;

Third – and even if European action is defined as necessary – it is still open to which extent this is the case.

With this it is getting clear that the principle of subsidiarity is immediately linked to a second principle, namely that of proportionality.

SURROUNDING

⇒ environment

TRAVELLER

Der Begriff als solcher lässt sich kaum übersetzen und gerade im internationalen Kontext sowie in historischer Perspektive ergeben sich immer wieder Unklarheiten. Zunächst handelt es sich grundsätzlich um eine Gruppe, die eher einzigartig für Irland zu sein scheint. Mittlerweile ist die Definition als eine ethnische Gruppe allgemein anerkannt und so wird bei der Übersetzung gerne auf Zigeuner, Landfahrer oder aber auch Sinti, Roma u.a. zurückgegriffen. Die Probleme damit sind freilich klar: Es handelt sich um Begriffe, die auch im Deutschen überholt sind oder aber sich auf bestimmte Gruppen beziehen, die mit denen der *traveller Gemeinschaft (travelling community, traveller community)* vergleichbar sein mögen, aber mehr eben auch nicht. *Nomadentum* ist sicherlich ein Gesichtspunkt, der beim Verständnis eine Rolle spielt, aber als Eigenschaft oder Verhaltensweise zu allgemein ist. In sehr weiter Perspektive ist eben für manche Gruppen der Wohnungslosen eine Art Nomadentum auch typisch. Eine weitere Schwierigkeit besteht darin, dass es mittlerweile "new traveller" gibt, die nicht einfach die nachrückende Generation bilden, sondern aus unterschiedlichen Lebenszusammenhängen kommen. Damit verbunden ist auch, dass es zunehmend *traveller-Gemeinschaften* auch in anderen Ländern gibt – relativ stark in Belgien und Schweden beispielsweise.

Und freilich ist der Begriff im Grunde trotz allem auch in ganz "harmloser" Verwendung zu finden und meint den Reisenden, den Wanderer – jemanden, der sich zu welchem Zwecke auch immer von einem Ort zu einem anderen bewegt. Nur ist diese doppelte Verwendung eines in dem einen Sinn allemal unklaren Begriffs problematisch. Dies wird deutlich bei dem Begriff der *Bahnhofsmission*, übersetzt als *Travellers' Aid Society.* Soweit denn diesem Wörterbuch Sprach-Definitionsmacht innewohnt, bevorzugt es den Begiff *passenger aid/passenger aid on the railway station* als Übersetzung für Bahnhofsmission.

UNIVERSALDIENST

"Dieser von den Gemeinschaftsinstitutionen entwickelte Begriff bezeichnet eine Reihe gemeinwohlorientierter Voraussetzungen, welche für bestimmte Dienste gemeinschaftsweit erfüllt sein sollten, z.B. durch die Telekommunikations- und Postunternehmen. Mit den sich daraus ergebenden Verpflichtungen soll der Zugang aller Bürger zu qualitativ hochwertigen Grundversorgungsleistungen gegen ein vertretbares Entgelt gesichert werden.“ *(EU-Glossar)*

Wohlfahrtsverband

Eine Abgrenzung und ebenso eine Übersetzung des Begriffes ist im Grunde nicht möglich.

Zum einen sind innerhalb der nationalen Systeme selbst sehr unterschiedliche “Konzepte“ von Organisationen vorfindbar. Dies bezieht sich auf die unterschiedlichen Rechtsformen (Vereine mit und ohne Steuerbefreiung im deutschen System als verbreitete Form, Stiftungen, Religionsgemeinschaften mit ihrem Sonderstatus u.a.) und vielleicht mehr noch auf die politisch-ideologischen Konzepte und Vorstellungen. Bei diesem Aspekt geht es dann um grundsätzliche Weltanschauungsfragen ebenso wie um Fragen in Einzelbereichen wie die Stellung gegenüber beispielsweise der Abtreibung. Aber auch Fragen der politischen Organisationsweise sind hier zu nennen – die unterschiedliche Sicht auf die Rolle des Staates oder etwa die Organisationsweise – Zentralismus, Föderalismus, Begrenzung auf dezentrale, bewusst klein-gehaltene Organisationen und Verfahren oder die Einbindung unabhängig bleibender Organisationen in Netzwerke können als Stichworte die Verschiedenheit kennzeichnen.

Zum anderen ist hier auf die Unterschiede zwischen den Ländern hinzuweisen. Auch hier sind wieder die verschiedenen Ebenen angesprochen wie die Organisationsweise – beispielsweise die in Deutschland unvorstellbar weite Verbreitung der Gesellschaften mit beschränkter Haftung (“ltd“) in England oder der Kooperativen in Frankreich und Italien – oder die politisch-ideologische Ausrichtung, die natürlich sichtbar eng mit dem vorgenannten Aspekt verbunden ist, aber ebenso darüber hinaus geht – die eher philanthropische Orientierung der englischen *charities* ist sicherlich etwas ganz anderes als der weltanschauliche Anspruch der in der BAGFW zusammengeschlossenen Verbände in Deutschland. Wichtig ist dabei auch, dass schon die jeweils zu wählenden Begriffe – selbst bei Gleichheit des Stammes – problematisch, weil schwer übersetzbar sind. Philanthropie und *philantrophy* klingen nahezu gleich und scheinen sich mehr als ähnlich, stehen aber für recht unterschiedliche Verständnisse. Und dies ist mit anderen Bereichen wie den genannten Kooperativen, aber ebenso mit einigen "Aufgabenbeschreibungen" der Fall.

Als möglicher sinnvoller "Sammelbegriff" wird eben derjenige der Wohlfahrtsverbände in der deutschen Sprache und derjenige der *welfare associations* in der englischen Sprache vorgeschlagen. Andere mögliche Begriffe wie beispielsweise derjenige der Agentur/*agency* sind hingegen problematisch: hierbei kann es sich um solche im Wohlfahrtsbereich handeln; dies ist allerdings in keiner Weise zwingend oder auch nur nahe liegend. Ähnliches gilt für Nicht-Regierungs Organisationen, gemeinnützige Organisationen u.a.m.

In diesem Zusammenhang ist zumindest der Hinweis auf die ⇒ civil society bedeutsam, denn auf die eine oder andere Weise sind die Wohlfahrtsverbände – fasst man sie in einem weiten Verständnis – sicherlich auch als deren Elemente anzusehen.

Insgesamt gilt, dass in allen Mitgliedstaaten der EU eine Vielfalt von Organisationen zu finden ist, die dem deutschen Verständnis nach als Wohlfahrtsverband anzusehen wären oder aber diesen ähnlich sind. Deren Beurteilung und Einordnung muss anerkennen, dass es in allen Ländern den Grundgedanken von Organisationen im Sozialbereich gibt, die auf freiwilliger Basis Zusammenschlüsse gründen und Aktivitäten entwickeln, die ihren Grund in Solidarität, partikularen Interessen, weltanschaulichen Ansätzen etc.

haben, ohne auf Profit ausgerichtet zu sein. Ein einheitliches EUropäisches Verständnis und Konzept existiert aber, wie festgestellt, nicht – doch große, über das ganze Land und in allen sozialen Feldern arbeitende Organisationen bestehen wohl in allen Ländern, wie es überall auch kleine, lokale Selbsthilfegruppen gibt. Der entscheidende Unterschied liegt wohl eher in

* den vorherrschenden ideologischen Mustern der zentralen Organisationen (z.B. die nach wie vor dominante Rolle der Kirche wie in Irland, der 'Säulenorganisationen' in den Niederlanden o.ä.),
* ihrer Rolle im Gesamtsystem, nicht zuletzt ihre Rücksicherung in einer *governance*-Struktur mit betonter Subsidiaritätsgeltung,
* der – vor allem durch die vorgenannten Faktoren bedingten und historisch entstandenen – vorherrschenden Orientierung auf eine Anwalts-, Dienstleistungs-, Avantgarde- oder Werte-Schutzfunktion,
* der Nähe zum gesellschaftlichen Wirtschaftsprozess, die nicht allein den Finanzierungsrahmen bestimmt, sondern vor allem auch (a) die Ausrichtung der Aktivitäten (z.B. 'Beschäftigungsgesellschaften' in der BRD) und (b) die Organisationsform (z.B. die große Bedeutung der Kooperativen und Vereine auf Gegenseitigkeit in Frankreich).